THE WRITER'S HANDBOOK
12 Workshops for Effective Writing

FOR SOCIAL WORKERS

COMPOSE FEARLESSLY · EDIT RUTHLESSLY ·

Write to Learn

Ordering Information
Contact us at www.thewriterstoolkit.com

THE WRITER'S HANDBOOK

12 Workshops for Effective Writing

FOR SOCIAL WORKERS

Dona J. Young

Contributions by
Andrea Tamburro
Marshelia Harris

The Writer's Handbook: 12 Workshops for Effective Writing

Dona J. Young
Contributions by Andrea Tamburro and Marshelia Harris

Writer's Toolkit Publishing LLC
www.wtkpublishing.com

Cover design by Nanc Ashby
www.saveldesign.com

© February 11, 2015, by Writer's Toolkit Publishing LLC, Ogden Dunes, Indiana.

ISBN-13: 978-0692380994
ISBN-10: 069238099X

Third printing.

The authors and editors have used their best efforts to ensure that that the information presented in this book was accurate at the time for publication.

Printed in the United States.
This book is printed on acid-free paper.

Writer's Toolkit Publishing LLC
www.wtkpublishing.com

To the caring social workers

who dedicate their lives to helping others

About the Authors

Dona J. Young, MA, teaches professional writing at Indiana University, Northwest campus. Young also designs and facilitates corporate writing programs. She earned an MA in education from The University of Chicago, a certificate from the Teacher Education Program (TEP) at The Chicago Institute for Psychoanalysis, and a BA in sociology from Northern Illinois University. She is the author of _Business Communication and Writing_ (Writer's Toolkit Publishing, 2012), _Business English: Writing for the Global Workplace_ (McGraw-Hill Higher Education, 2008), and _Foundations of Business Communication_ (McGraw-Hill/Irwin, 2006), among others. Young believes that writing is a powerful learning tool and that learning shapes our lives.

Andrea Tamburro, MSW and EdD, is a member of the Shawnee Tribe and is the Bachelor of Social Work Program Director at Indiana University, Northwest campus. She teaches policy, research, and practice. She earned her education doctorate from Simon Fraser University in British Columbia, Canada, and her master of social work through the University of Iowa. Tamburro's main research area is Indigenous social work education; her practice areas include child welfare, mental health, domestic violence, and criminal justice. Tamburro contributed to every chapter.

Marshelia Harris, MSW, is the field coordinator for the Bachelor of Social Work Program in the Indiana University School of Social Work, Northwest campus. She teaches policy, administration, and child welfare across the bachelor and master of social work programs. Harris received her MSW from Indiana University. She is a licensed child welfare specialist with several years of administrative experience in social services, case management, and clinical services. Harris has also managed parenting and non-parenting youth programs, developed new programs, and facilitated training. Harris is pursuing a doctorate in social work at St. Catherine University – University of St. Thomas. Harris contributed to Chapter 10, "Writing Effective Grants and Proposals."

Brief Contents

About the Method

As a supplement to *The Writer's Handbook*, this book presents 12 workshops that develop editing skills needed to produce effective writing.

Each workshop can be completed in about an hour. The workshops are sequenced so that one concept leads to the next, simplifying the learning process. The workshops are designed to present a minimum of theory followed by practice. For more detailed explanations, refer to *The Writer's Handbook: A Guide for Social Workers*.

- The first step is gaining control of the writing process. Once you compose as a separate activity from editing, you are ready to build editing skills. Writing your ideas freely is critical to the entire process.

- The next step is working on the mechanics of writing. Punctuation is the key to effective editing because you focus on the *sentence core:* the most basic and powerful unit of editing.

- Though you can work on your own, you gain more value by working with a partner or in a small group. By discussing principles, you are more likely to apply them.

Once you can compose freely, each editing principle that you apply improves your results. By gaining control of the sentence core, you gain control of the quality of your writing. By working in teams, you view solutions from several different perspectives, gaining insight and learning principles at a deeper level.

Principles of one topic are linked to principles of another topic—that is why it sometimes feels difficult to make progress. This book helps you focus on the sentence core so that you readily learn to make decisions that lead to accurate, clear, and concise writing. As you learn each new principle, your editing skills improve and, thus, the quality of your writing improves.

These workshops organize essential topics to accelerate learning so that you develop proficiency. This approach simplifies the learning process, but your ultimate challenge is to apply what you are learning in your own writing. Only you can do that.

Write to Learn—Edit to Clarify

Process Messages

To support the learning process, your professor may periodically ask you to send a process message. Think of a process message as a *progress message* or *report* in which you share your insights and discuss your learning process, for example: *What are you learning and how are your applying it?*

Here are some details about how to send a professionally written e-mail message.

1. **For all e-mail messages,** use a *greeting* that includes the *recipient's name*; also include a *closing*.

```
┌─────────────────────────────────────────────────────────────────────┐
│  ┌─────────┐    To ...    Professor Harris                           │
│  │  Send   │    Cc ...                                               │
│  └─────────┘    Subject:  Process Message: Commas                    │
│  ─────────────────────────────────────────────────────────────────  │
│                                                                       │
│  Hi Professor Harris,                                                 │
│                                                                       │
│  Attached is the worksheet on comma usage. Though I still have        │
│  questions about comma placement, I no longer place commas based on   │
│  where I think a reader should pause.                                 │
│                                                                       │
│  The more exercises I complete, the more confident I feel. I am even  │
│  going back to edit my journals, putting in commas and identifying the│
│  rules.                                                               │
│                                                                       │
│  Thank you for your assistance with this assignment.                  │
│                                                                       │
│  All the best,                                                        │
│                                                                       │
│  Jasmine                                                              │
└─────────────────────────────────────────────────────────────────────┘
```

2. Always follow standard rules of grammar, punctuation, spelling, and capitalization.

3. Avoid using abbreviations and *never* use text message language in e-mail messages. (For example, the personal pronoun *I* is always capitalized.)

4. When you reply to a message, leave the *thread*. By leaving the history, your reader understands the context in which to reply to your message.

5. Update the subject line so that the recipient can file your message effectively.

6. Include white space (a blank line) after the salutation, between paragraphs, and before your closing. By leaving white space between paragraphs, you do not need to indent paragraphs: block all lines at the left.

7. When you send assignments as e-mail attachments, label your work correctly by including *your name* in the file name; for example, "Tamburro.Assignment 1."

8. Before sending your assignment, compare your work with the instructions to make sure you have completed the assignment correctly.

9. Respect all due dates: if you need an extension, *ask for it in advance.*

10. *Work independently:* try to figure things out on your own before asking questions. This approach prepares you for what will be expected in your profession.

11. Save and file all class communications; keep track of all of your assignments, feedback, and grades.

12. When you have an urgent message for your instructor, use a subject line that reflects your question or request so that your message does not remain in a cue with ungraded papers.

13. If you are angry or upset, set your e-mail aside; re-read it the next day when you are feeling calmer to decide if you want to revise it before sending it: *When in doubt, do not send it.*

14. Finally, keep human elements of online communication alive by respecting your classmates and professor: *following protocol is one way to show respect.*

In summary, adapt to what is expected:

o   Know best practices and follow them.

o   Use greetings and closings when you write an e-mail.

o   *Never use text messaging language.*

o   Label your assignments correctly.

o   Try to figure things out before you ask for help.

Become confident in your ability to communicate effectively—the more you put into learning, the more value you gain.

You become what you learn.

—John Dewey

Contents

Notes

1

Get Started Quickly

In this workshop, you gain insight into the writing process and how to overcome writing blocks. You also learn tools that you can apply as you develop a writing strategy.

In preparation for this workshop (or as follow-up to it), read Chapter 7, "Writing as Process," in *The Writer's Handbook: A Guide for Social Workers* (2014).

Start by taking the learning inventory below, and then work through the activities on your own or with a partner.

Workshop 1 Inventory

Instructions: Answer the questions below; evaluate each question on a scale of 1 to 5.

  1 = **Never**   3 = **Sometimes**   5 =**Always**

Do you do any of the following?

1. Do you try to figure things out in your head before you put the words on the page?

2. Do you try to write your first draft so that it is good enough to turn in?

3. If your first draft is not good, do you think there is something wrong with your skills?

4. Do you correct grammar, spelling, and word usage as you compose?

5. Do you lose your train of thought because you are correcting and revising as you are writing?

6. Do you avoid the task until the due date is in sight, when the adrenaline kicks in?

7. Are you critical of your writing and think everyone writes better than you do?

8. Do you shut down and avoid the task completely?

9. Do you finish documents without connecting your purpose with your reader's needs?

10. Is your writing full of quotes or information you have copied from another source?

Note: When you have finished, turn to page 209 for the key to this inventory.

Everyone has challenges with writing, even the best writers. By becoming more aware of your writing experiences—both negative and positive—you make room for a way of thinking about writing that supports your growth.

The activity below assists you in gaining insight into what works and what doesn't work about your current writing process.

Activity 1.1

What Is Difficult about Writing?

In a small group or with a partner, explore the following, jotting down key points:

1. What are the things about writing that challenge you?

2. Do you put off writing tasks until the last minute? If so, why?

3. What do you think about your ability to write? What kinds of experiences have shaped your feelings about writing?

4. What kinds of skills and abilities does writing enhance? What do you like about writing?

5. How can writing help you grow?

Take notes, as you might be asked to write a paper about this topic.

Activity 1.2

Do You Have a Writing Block?

When you get stuck, you may think that you have writer's block. However, writer's block occurs most frequently with professional writers. Instead, you are more likely to have a form of editor's block or critic's block.

- *Editor's Block Type A*: You edit as you compose, and your ideas get jammed in your head or dissolve before they reach the page.

- *Editor's Block Type B:* You do not proofread or edit your work before you send it out. Since you are unsure of what to correct or revise, you hold your breath and press the *send* button.

- *Critic's Block:* Every time you think of writing, you remember all of your failures and forget about your successes. You put off writing tasks as long as possible because the writing process feels intimidating.

To take care of **Editor's Block Type A**, separate composing from editing: you will see an immediate difference in your writing. You will produce more in less time; you will also feel less frustrated and, ultimately, more confident. Use planning and composing tools such as mind mapping and page mapping.

To overcome **Editor's Block Type B**, take the time to proofread and edit each piece of writing that you produce. By developing your skills, you will understand the principles that lead to correct, clear, and concise writing. Then be vigilant as you edit your writing.

To overcome **Critic's Block**, accept that no one writes perfectly and everyone has challenges. Think of criticism as feedback that leads to growth. Turn off any messages that are self-defeating. With practice, you will build your writing skills: It's about progress, not perfection. *Perfect writing does not exist.* Do your best, and then let go of the rest.

Which types of writing blocks do you have? What changes do you need to make to improve your writing skills? List at least 2 or 3 changes below:

Writing Tools

Use the following techniques to manage the writing process so that you compose more fluently: mind mapping, page mapping, and freewriting.

Mind Mapping   This form of brainstorming allows you to get your ideas on the page in a quick, spontaneous way.

1.   First, choose your topic.

2.   Next, write your topic in a "bubble" in the middle of the page.

3.   Finally, brainstorm ideas and cluster them around your topic.

Here's an example of mind mapping in response to the question, "What is my dream job?"

Page Mapping   Put your main ideas or key points from your scratch outline or mind map along the side of a blank page. Then fill in the details by using each key point as the topic for a focused-writing activity.

Since the topic above is self-reflective, you may want to turn your key points—or side headings—into questions, for example:

My Dream Job

- *What benefits do I need?*
- *Where am I going to focus my job search?*
- *What kinds of jobs will I consider?*
- *What is most important to me?*
- *What do I need to prepare for my search?*
- *What is holding me back from finishing my career portfolio?*

Activity 1.3

Mind Map

Instructions: Identify a topic or a problem that you are working on. Spend about 3 minutes doing a mind map. (If you wish, use your mind map to create a page map.)

Note: You can find free mind mapping software online by doing an Internet search.

Activity 1.4

Freewriting | Focused Writing

Instructions: Spend 10 to 15 minutes getting your words down freely: do not correct your writing or edit your thoughts. To *freewrite*, start writing whatever comes to your mind, putting your words down in a freeform, stream of consciousness way. For focused writing, select a topic first and then stay on that topic for the allotted time.

These activities enhance your ability to compose freely: when you compose, turn off your "editor."

Activity 1.5

Fishbone Diagram

Also known as a *cause-and-effect diagram* or an *Ishikawa diagram*, this brainstorming tool gets at primary reasons. Start by identifying your problem, then identify major components of it. For each component, ask *why* five times.

For a simpler version (as illustrated below), simply identify one issue and then ask why five times.

Problem statement: I can't meet my writing deadline.

Why? Because I am wasting a lot of time, putting it off instead of working on it.

Why? Because I feel stressed every time I think about it.

Why? Because I don't know how to start.

Why? Because I'm not confident about my topic.

Why? Because I haven't done my research.

Next step: Start my research now.

Problem statement:

_____

*Why?*_____

*Why?*_____

*Why?*_____

*Why?*_____

*Why?*_____

*Next Step*_____

Note: If you find the *fishbone brainstorming technique* effective, do an Internet search to find a variety of alternatives.

What variations have you found? How will you adapt this tool for your own use? Is this a tool that could be used effectively in task groups?

Templates

You can use a template for small tasks as well as large ones. Think of a template as a prompt to get your ideas flowing and help you organize them.

For e-mail, the **CAET** template offers a basic structure:

C	**Connect**	Use a greeting to create a personal link with your reader.
A	**Act**	State action needed at the beginning of the message.
E	**Explain**	Include only details relevant to your reader.
T	**Thank**	Thank your reader, as appropriate.

As you compose a paper, use the **peer model** to prompt your thinking; as you revise, use it to develop your topic adequately with specific evidence and examples.

P	What is the *purpose*? What are the *key points?* Why are they relevant?
E	What *evidence* demonstrates the main points? What are the facts and details?
E	What *explanation* or *examples* do readers need to understand the evidence and its significance?
R	How can you *resolve* your thesis for your readers? What are the key points for your *recap*? What are your conclusions and *recommendations*?

Academic Writing: Summaries and Arguments

Academic writing is a type of writing that is formal, which can feel intimidating. When writers lack confidence, they may make the mistake of plagiarizing: cutting and pasting the words of others works against the learning process and shows a lack of respect for all. The way to build skill is to spend more time writing, and the first step is learning to write a **summary**.

Summarizing in your own words what others are saying is the starting point for building critical thinking and writing skills. As you do your research, stop at critical points to write key ideas *from your own recollection*. In other words, take your eyes off of your sources and do not look at your notes. Once you have summarized key ideas, compare them with the sources and notate your references.

Writing a summary is the foundation for writing an **argument.** When you write an argument, use evidence to support your position.

- What is your position? Write a thesis that expresses a position that can be argued. (For example, an *opinion* could not be the basis for an argument.)

- What points are you making? What evidence are you using? What conclusions are you drawing?

- What are the underlying assumptions in the articles you have chosen? (For example, "Child neglect is bad and children who are neglected should be removed from their parents.")

- What evidence is confusing or lacking or unsubstantiated? What are the *gaps* in thinking or in the logic of arguments?

- What are counter-arguments to this issue? (For example, "Children are more damaged by the foster care system than in some neglectful environments.")

- How can you improve the argument? Will your evidence convince a skeptic?

When you argue a point, do not use the first person, such as *I agree* or *I disagree*, but rather use phrases such as "the argument" or "the author":

This paper analyzes / discusses / examines / investigates . . .

The thesis / premise / central issue is . . . The authors argue that . . .

This study examines . . . Some findings / conclusions are . . .

The data suggest . . . The authors assume that . . . Their research validates . . .

Their research does not support . . . Based on research, the authors conclude . . .

Consensus among the researchers includes agreement about . . .

Since academic writing has its own style, start developing your academic voice by using **sentence prompts**.

Sentence Prompts

Using sentence prompts is a legitimate way to structure your ideas and is distinctly different from plagiarizing. Sentence prompts can help ease you into building your academic vocabulary. The following example was adapted from the University of Manchester's Academic Phrasebank, http://**www.phrasebank.manchester.ac.uk/**:

Jones (2011)	found observed	distinct significant considerable major only slight	differences between X and Y.

Activity 1.6

Sentence Prompts

1. **Instructions:** Visit the University of Manchester's website, Academic Phrasebank, http://**www.phrasebank.manchester.ac.uk**, and summarize a few points that you learned about academic writing.

2. **Instructions:** Select a published journal article. Rather than reading the article for meaning, analyze the writer's style and highlight generic phrases that can be used as sentence prompts.

Activity 1.7

Process Message

Instructions: Write your professor a process message (see page xi) summarizing a few points that you have learned about academic writing and how you can build your skills along with any other information you wish to share or discuss.

Workshop Assignments

Application 1.1

What Is Difficult about Writing?

Instructions: Write a short paper discussing your history as a writer.

Start by mind mapping the question or by completing a scratch outline. Next provide more detail: sit down and write. Do not edit your writing as you compose—just get your ideas on the page.

Writing about your experiences opens the process so that you can make substantial progress. By honestly revisiting some experiences, you can let go of them as well as unproductive ways of thinking that hold you back. As an ancient saying tells us,

If you hold it in, it will destroy you; if you let it out, it will free you.

Now go back and read out loud what you wrote. *What do you see and hear?*

Application 1.2

Goals and Objectives

Instructions: Review your syllabus for this class and the table of contents for your book, *The Writer's Handbook: A Guide for Social Workers* (2014). What goals and objectives would you like to achieve as a result of taking this class?

- A *goal* is a broad statement of what you intend to achieve.
- An *objective* is a narrow, precise statement of a specific and measurable action that you intend to achieve.

Write 2 goals below along with 2 objectives and tasks to support each goal.

1. Goal 1:

    a. Objective:

        i. Task

        ii. Task

    b. Objective:

        i. Task

        ii. Task

2. Goal 2:

    a. Objective:

        i. Task

        ii. Task

    b. Objective:

        i. Task

        ii. Task

By the way, social workers include objectives and goals when they write grants and proposals. As you write your personal goals, you are also developing your skills for writing goals and objectives for grant proposal writing.

Application 1.3

Journaling

Journaling is reflective writing. Social workers reflect on their work with client systems in their case notes, in staff meetings, and in supervision.

Instructions: Start a journal following the *2 x 4 method*: 2 pages, 4 times a week.

As you journal, you gain insight into who you are, what motivates you, and how to make important changes.

1.   When you journal, write freely: do not stop to correct your writing.

2.   Stay organized—get a notebook or start a file on your computer or tablet.

3.   Write for 10 minutes or 2 pages, pouring whatever is on your mind onto the pages of your journal.

Journaling helps you find your voice as you gain the experience of using writing as a problem-solving tool. *Write 2 pages in your journal at least 4 times a week, and you will make progress.*

Application 1.4

Work Journal

Instructions: Start a work journal, using a reflective tool such as the DEAL Model (See pages 84 – 87 in *The Writer's Handbook: A Guide for Social Workers*).

The **DEAL Model** is a three-step process to enhance critical reflection on experiences to gain deeper insight (Ash & Clayton, 2004). One goal is to gain insight into how experiences are integrated with principles gained from academic content.

Here are the three steps:

D =   **Describe** a specific experience.

E =   **Examine** it closely.

AL =   **Articulate Learning** – *What did I learn? How will I apply it?*

Keep your work journal separate from your personal journal, using a separate notebook or file on your computer or tablet.

Pre-Assessment

Instructions: Go to **www.thewriterstoolkit.com** to take the skills assessment.

1. In the upper left corner, click on the *Skills Assessment* tab.

2. Print a copy of the assessment.

3. Spend a maximum of 15 minutes completing the assessment.

4. Give a copy of the completed assessment to your professor.*

*Once you take the pre-assessment, do not review it until you complete the book.

The assessment contains the following 3 parts:

Part A: Grammar

Part B: Punctuation

Part C: Word Usage

Based on how challenging the assessment was, please rate your knowledge of the following topics on a scale of 1 to 5: *1* means *little or no competence* and *5* means *complete competence*.

Part A. Grammar

Part B. Punctuation

Part C. Word Usage

Skill Profile

How did you score?

The assessment has a total of 100 points. For each incorrect answer, deduct 2 points.

		Score
Pretest 1: Grammar Skills	_____ incorrect (20 possible)	_____
Pretest 2: Punctuation Skills	_____ incorrect (20 possible)	_____
Pretest 3: Word Usage Skills	_____ incorrect (10 possible)	_____
Total:	_____	_____

For example, a total of 20 incorrect would equal a total score of 60 percent:

$$20 \times -2 = -40 \text{ from } 100$$

Time Management Tips for Writing

Whenever you write, you face the unknown, a daunting task for all. For your next project, use the following tips to get started on your project quickly and stay focused.

- Work backwards: Break your task into parts and then set internal deadlines, working backward from your due date. *The sooner you start, the more time you have.*

- Plan writing tasks into your calendar: Write when you are fresh and operating at maximum potential.

- Write about what is keeping you from tackling your projects head on. Freewrite or do a fishbone diagram (see pages 5 – 6). Start with the question, "What is keeping me from writing?"

- Set aside time specifically for research—ideas fuel creativity. If you haven't done your research, *why would you expect for words to flow?*

- Jot down ideas when you have them; keep a small notebook with you at all times.

- Use a template such as the PEER Model (see page 7). Fill in the parts you know first—let what you know lead you to what you need to discover. Once you start to solve a problem, answers begin to reveal themselves.

- Take a focused break by walking away from your task, literally. Walking is a meditative activity. (If you walk a dog, that's even better.) Insights often come when you detach yourself from intense problem solving but remain reflective.

- Identify your time wasters. *What keeps you from reaching your goals? Do you need to say "no" to activities or people who draw you away from your purpose?*

- Remain flexible. At times, you will have planned to work on a certain piece of your project, but instead feel tugged in a different direction. As long as you are focused on your project, *go with the flow*. Remaining flexible also pertains to outcomes.

- Take care of yourself—no excuses. By balancing your time and your diet, you help balance your life and keep stress manageable. Also, use self-talk in a positive and constructive way to embrace your challenges.

There is nothing to writing. All you do is sit down at a typewriter and bleed.

—Ernest Hemingway

References

Academic Phrasebank at http://www.phrasebank.manchester.ac.uk/

Ash, S., Clayton, P., & Moses, M. (2006). *Excerpts from teaching and learning through critical reflection: An instructor's guide.* Raleigh, NC: Author. [Model modified for social work by Lisa E. McGuire, Ph. D. & Kathy Lay, Ph.D. Indiana University School of Social Work.]

Young, D., Tamburro, A., and Harris, M. (2014). *The writer's handbook: A guide for social workers.* Ogden Dunes, IN: Writer's Toolkit Publishing LLC.

Notes

The Writer's Handbook: 12 Workshops for Effective Writing

2

Put Purpose First

With academic and professional writing, one mistake that a writer can make is to develop an answer that does not address the question at hand.

What is the question? If there is no question, then there is no answer.

—Gertrude Stein

Simply put, before you answer, understand the question. Understanding your question is an element of purpose: when your answer does not correspond with the question, readers lose interest and your writing loses credibility.

In this workshop, you explore purpose from broad and specific angles; you work on revising short messages, developing cohesive and coherent paragraphs, and gaining skill with paraphrasing and summarizing.

To prepare, review Chapter 9, "Cohesive Paragraphs and Transitions," *The Writer's Handbook: A Guide for Social Workers* (2014).

Workshop 2 Inventory

Instructions: Answer the questions below.

1. Give substantial background information before stating the purpose.   T/F
2. Answering a question starts with understanding the problem.   T/F
3. Readers want to know all of the details of *how* you decided on a course of action.   T/F
4. Shaping your writing for the audience and its expectations is part of purpose.   T/F
5. Three types of information to control are "old," "new," and "empty."   T/F
6. A writer's background thinking is considered empty information.   T/F
7. Effective paragraphs are coherent, which means that sentences can be about different topics as long as each sentence makes sense.   T/F
8. In e-mail messages, your subject line should always reflect your purpose.   T/F

Note: See page 209 for the key to this inventory.

Purpose: Problem and Plan

Have you ever written a message or even a paper that did *not* respond to what the reader really wanted to know? This wasted effort occurs often across all lines of professional and academic writing. As part of your process, make it a priority to understand the question *before* you develop your answer.

Here are some questions you can ask to become clear about your purpose:

- What is the question being asked?
  - What is the problem?
- Who is my audience?
  - What are their expectations?
  - How can I shape my response to their needs and questions?
- What are the guidelines and instructions that I need to follow?
- What kind of writing is needed: *A summary? An argument?*

If you use writing to clarify your thinking, you may start writing simply to get your rough-draft thinking on paper. Before you get too far into your process, however, shape your writing in response to the above questions. Otherwise, you may waste valuable time and energy doing the "wrong assignment."

Whether you are writing a social history, a grant proposal, or an academic assignment, first review the guidelines. Guidelines help you understand the purpose, goals, and ground rules. For example, when writing a grant, describe the need or purpose and then explain your project clearly. In essence, you will be establishing *why* your project is important before going into detail about how you plan to address the need.

Purpose provides context for your writing, making the details meaningful. With professional writing, readers want the key points and conclusions as quickly as possible: how you arrived at your conclusions may not be important. In contrast, most academic writing is evidence based: readers need the information that led to your conclusions.

In professional writing and academic writing, readers appreciate knowing conclusions *before* reading the detail and supporting research. For example, *reading for meaning* is different from *reading for entertainment*. When readers need to work hard to see where comments are leading, fine details can become frustrating and the motivation to continue reading is reduced.

Let us next look at a process for revising short messages before and then work with information flow, paragraphs, and voice.

Purpose and Process

As you compose, understanding purpose often comes as a flash of insight. Once you write a sentence that clarifies what you want to say, use your insight as a signal that you are ready to start editing.

1. Cut and paste the key sentence to the beginning of your message.
2. Then delete unnecessary, irrelevant detail.

Writing is a discovery process: as your thinking becomes clear, your purpose becomes clear. Compose freely; when you edit, cut information that is obvious and avoid using the word *purpose*. For example, your first draft might include the following:

> Hi Professor Harris,
>
> My name is Pam, and I am in your SW351 class. My purpose for writing you is to let you know that I cannot turn in my research paper that is due today. Over the weekend, I went to visit my sister, who lives in Indianapolis. Because my paper was almost complete, I didn't bring my laptop with me. Then the weather got bad, so I needed to stay there another day. Because I left my laptop at home, I could not finish my paper. If I could send you my paper tomorrow, I would be so thankful.
>
> Sincerely,
>
> Pam Halpert

When you revise your message, remove the word *purpose* along with information that is either obvious or the reader does not need to know:

> Hi Professor Harris,
>
> I am in your SW351 class and am requesting extra time to complete my research paper.
>
> Over the weekend, I went out of town without my computer and was unable to return home due to bad weather. I now have access to my computer, and my paper is almost completed. Would it be possible for me to turn it in tomorrow?
>
> Thank you for considering my request.
>
> Pam Halpert

Activity 2.1

Analyze the Revision

Instructions: Take a moment to analyze the difference between the two messages on page 19—what changes did Pam make on the revision?

_____

_____

Activity 2.2

Revise for Purpose

Instructions: As you read the e-mail below, take special note of where in the message the writer's purpose finally becomes clear. Write your revision at the top of the next page.

1. Identify the key point.
2. Bring the key point to the beginning of the message.
3. Cut irrelevant, empty information.

Dear Mr. Scott:

My name is Dwight Schrute, and I recently met an associate of yours while I was attending a paper convention. Her name is Pam Beesly, and she suggested that I write you because you are the person in charge of hiring at your office. To give you a little background about myself, I am currently working for Acme Paper Company, one of your competitors. While I realize that this could work for me, it could also work against me. My purpose in writing you is to find out if it would be possible to meet with you in person to discuss any openings that you may have and consider the talent that I could bring to your company. I would be pleased to send you my resume or come in for an interview at your earliest convenience. I look forward to hearing from you.

Sincerely,

Dwight Schrute

Activity 2.2: Revision

_____

_____

_____

_____

_____

_____

Note: When you are finished, see the bottom of page 22 for a possible revision.

Information Flow

Information flow—the order in which you present ideas—affects the quality of your writing. Let us start by breaking information into three broad categories:

- *Old Information*: familiar information.
- *New Information*: unfamiliar information.
- *Empty Information*: irrelevant information.

Writing that flows well tends to mix old information effectively with new information, with the familiar introducing the unfamiliar.

- Old information tends to be global, and new information tends to be specific.
- Old information anchors new information, which extends the reader's knowledge.

Right now, information flow may be a new concept. Work with this concept until you get a feel for identifying the difference between old and new information. In the following examples, old information is italicized:

New to *old* information flow:

The national budget crisis will be *the topic of my next paper*.

A new construction project has begun *at the corner of State and Lake*.

Chocolate, sardines, and coconut milk are on *my shopping list*.

Can you see how the beginning of each of the above sentences sounds abrupt? For example, doesn't "chocolate, sardines, and goat's milk" sound abrupt in comparison to "my shopping list"? Here are same sentences with the information flow reversed:

Old to new information flow:

My next paper will analyze the national budget crisis.

At the corner of State and Lake, a new construction project has begun.

My shopping list includes chocolate, sardines, and goat's milk.

Even in these short, simple sentences, can you see how the information flow affects readability? By beginning with the familiar, are the sentences more reader-friendly? Composing is messy; editing is the tidying up part. At times, you will need to cut and paste a key sentence to the beginning of a paragraph; at other times, you will need to cut and paste a key paragraph to another part of your document.

Here is a revision for Activity 2.2 on page 20:

Dear Mr. Scott:

At a recent convention, Pam Beesly suggested that I write you about opportunities at your company.

As an experienced sales representative, I have a passion for sales and can bring an excellent understanding of how to leverage products at your company. My résumé is attached.

I look forward to hearing from you. In the meantime, you can reach me at 570-272-1212.

Best regards,

Dwight Schrute

Is the revised message more accessible? How does the tone change? What other changes improve the message?

Cohesive and Coherent Paragraphs

Paragraphs break information into manageable chunks, playing a vital role in making ideas easily accessible. In fact, readers dread seeing one long paragraph, knowing instantly that reading it will be a chore. Effective paragraphs are *cohesive* and *coherent*.

- *Cohesive* paragraphs develop only *one main idea* or *key point*.
- *Coherent* paragraphs develop the main idea through a *logical flow of ideas*.

To edit a paragraph so that it is cohesive, first identify its *topic sentence*. Then ensure that each sentence in the paragraph supports the topic, creating a *topic string*.

- A *topic sentence* gives an overview of the paragraph; a topic sentence is broad and general.
- A *topic string* is a series of sentences that develop the main idea of the topic sentence. Each sentence extends the main idea, giving specific information that illustrates the central idea of the topic sentence. These sentences may include evidence that supports the topic sentence.

Here is a step-by-step process for editing paragraphs:

1. Identify your topic sentence. Select the sentence that best captures the broader, more general topic that the rest of the paragraph develops through specifics.
2. Bring your topic sentence to the beginning of the paragraph.
3. Screen each sentence in the topic string to make sure that it develops some element of the topic sentence.
4. Cut sentences that do not fit or use them to start a new paragraph.

When the topic changes, so does the paragraph. Once you have enough experience writing, you will readily identify when the topic changes and paragraphing will become a natural part of composing. When you edit, you will structure the content to make your paragraphs *cohesive* and *coherent*.

Let us first look at how to develop a cohesive paragraph and then how to revise it so that it is coherent.

Cohesive Paragraphs

Cohesive paragraphs develop one main idea, and this idea controls the content of the paragraph. The sentence that presents the main idea or topic in the most effective way is called the *topic sentence*. Though the topic sentence can appear anywhere in a paragraph, the most effective placement is generally at the beginning as the first or second sentence.

For a paragraph to be cohesive, each sentence in the paragraph must relate to the topic sentence, thereby developing a *topic string*. A sentence that does not relate to the topic should be cut or used to start a new paragraph.

After you complete the exercise below, you examine how to revise the information flow of a paragraph, making it coherent.

Activity 2.3

Revise for Cohesion

Instructions: For the following paragraph about health and safety programs, use the following as a guide to revising the paragraph:

1. Which sentence is the topic sentence?

2. Which sentences develop the topic string?

3. Which sentence or sentences should be removed so that the paragraph is cohesive?

By implementing health and safety programs for employees, an agency can gain multiple rewards. Reduced absenteeism, increased productivity, and improved employee moral are often the results of a comprehensive health program. In addition, substantial savings in reduced insurance claims and premiums is another result of having a health program. Our agency implemented a health and safety program and had effective results. In addition, the families of the employees appreciated the program as much as our employees did.

Note: See page 210 for the key to this activity.

Coherent Paragraphs

A coherent paragraph has a logical flow of ideas: one idea leads seamlessly to the next without gaps in meaning that cause a reader to struggle to find meaning.

To develop a coherent paragraph, apply principles of information flow (see page 21): use *old, familiar information* to introduce *new, unfamiliar information*.

The old information relates to the main idea (topic) of the paragraph; the new information extends the reader's understanding. Building old to new information flow helps readers make connections; familiar ideas ease readers into the unfamiliar.

The paragraph above about health and safety programs sounds choppy (and thus incoherent) because sentences begin with new information that is then attached to old information. To improve the flow, edit each sentence, using old information to introduce the new.

Here's how to achieve effective information flow:

- Move the topic *health and safety programs* (old information) to the beginning of each sentence.
- Move information about *rewards* (new information) to the end of each sentence.

The topic string then flows from the topic of "health and safety programs" (which is a constant topic) to new information or "rewards" (which varies or expands). In the examples that follow, **old information is in bold** and *new information in italics*.

Topic Sentence:	**By implementing health and safety programs for employees**, *an agency can gain multiple rewards.*

Example 1

New to **Old**:	*Reduced absenteeism, increased productivity, and improved employee moral are often the results* **of a comprehensive health program.**
Old to *New*:	**A comprehensive health program** *reduces absenteeism, increases productivity, and improves employee morale.*

Example 2

New to **Old**:	In addition, *substantial savings in reduced insurance claims and premiums* is **another result of having a health program.**
Old *New*:	In addition, **a health program results** *in substantial savings by reducing insurance claims and premiums.*

Now, here is the same paragraph revised to have *old to new information flow:*

Revised: **By implementing health and safety programs for employees**, *an agency can reap multiple rewards.* **A comprehensive health program** *reduces absenteeism, increases productivity, and improves employee morale.* In addition, **a health program** *results in substantial savings by reducing insurance claims and premiums.*

You may notice that the topic "health and safety programs" changes subtly in its form though not in its meaning. This variation adds creativity and keeps the reader engaged.

Revising Paragraphs

Here are some steps you can take when revising paragraphs:

- *Print out a copy.* Writing sometimes reads differently in hard copy from the way it reads on the screen.

- *Have a peer read it.* Ask for specific changes that you can make to upgrade the quality of your writing.

- *Keep an open mind.* Others will see things that you cannot; expand your perspective by trying new ideas, even if they feel uncomfortable at first. You can always toss them out if they don't work.

In academic writing, aim to write paragraphs that are about 4 to 8 sentences in length: one topic sentence and at least three sentences to explain, expand, and support the topic sentence.

When you write especially long paragraphs—those longer than a third of a page—see if you can break the information into chunks that are more manageable to process.

Sentence length is also important. So that your writing is reader friendly, keep your sentences to 25 words or fewer. Readers are not impressed with writing when they forget the beginning of a sentence by the time they finally reach the end of it.

Finally, if you have a belief that your writing must impress to be effective, readjust your thinking. The logical and insightful development of your thesis will impress your reader; complicated writing only complicates the issue.

Activity 2.4

Revise Information Flow

Instructions: Follow these steps to revise the information flow in the paragraph below:

1. Identify the topic sentence and topic string.

2. If a sentence is not part of the topic string, remove it.

3. Adjust information flow so that old information (or the main topic) introduces new information.

Our agency implemented a health and safety program and had positive results. Employees were encouraged to take an active role to prevent disease in our new program. A health center was provided by this innovative program where employees could conveniently get daily aerobic exercise and weight training. Periodic tests to monitor blood pressure, cholesterol, and triglycerides were also provided as part of the package. Some employees did not set aside the time to participate in the program. Within one year, a significant percentage of employees had reduced risk factors for heart disease.

Note: See page 210 for the key to this activity.

Your Voice

Do you ever find yourself copying parts of sentences from another's writing? Or perhaps taking a few sentences, changing a few words? These are examples of plagiarism.

Writers plagiarize when they do not feel confident with their own writing. The way to feel confident about writing is to find your voice: the way to find your voice is to write from your own experience about your own ideas and insights until your words flow. *Never copy any part of someone else's writing*—even when you take notes, put ideas in your own words, keeping track of your source for a possible citation.

Voice is an element of all types of writing, not just creative or personal writing, but professional and academic writing as well. In fact, you will find that your voice changes according to the type of writing that you are doing: *personal*, *professional*, or *academic*. Each of these types of writing involves using pronouns effectively; here is a preview of what you will learn in Chapter 5, "Use Pronouns Correctly":

- When you write from your *personal voice*, you are expressing your feelings and opinions. Use your personal voice when you write in a journal. When you speak from your personal voice, feel free to use the personal pronoun "I" (which, by the way, is always capitalized).

- When you write from your *professional voice*, you are connecting with readers through simple, clear, concise writing. Use your professional voice when you write e-mail messages, business letters, and memos. Limit your use of the ***I* point of view**, shifting to the ***you* point of view** when possible.

- When you write from your *academic voice*, you are writing in the most formal way, taking ideas and concepts apart, analyzing data, decisions, positions, and actions as well as asking questions in a dispassionate, non-adversarial way. For the most part, use the **third person point of view**.

If you have not yet found your voice, stay committed to the process. By writing freely, you develop your ability to write as fluently as you speak. The next step is editing: shape your writing for your audience until your voice comes through.

Finding your voice is not a one-time event: *voice* is a process in which you reconnect with yourself, your topic, and your readers every time you sit down to write. Connecting with yourself and others is what makes writing challenging and also what turns writing into a powerful tool. As you gain insight, you enrich your understanding, growing as a writer and as a human being.

To find your voice, write freely: 2 pages, 4 times a week.

Summarizing and Paraphrasing

Incorporating the ideas of other writers is a critical element of academic writing. The only requirement is that you cite your source when you quote, summarize, or paraphrase another source.

- When you *paraphrase*, you are "translating" an original piece of writing but not copying any parts word for word. Paraphrasing is putting someone else's ideas in your own words so that you can explain how their ideas support or oppose your topic.

- When you *summarize*, you are putting the most important elements of the original writing into your own words.

If you are not confident about your writing skills, you may be tempted to copy or quote much material into your writing. Instead, as a writer, you need to develop your voice, which enables you to interpret information in your own words; here is how:

- To paraphrase or summarize, first read the original source.
- Write a few notes *in your own words* about what the author is saying.
- Next, put away the original source and write your summary.

After you write your summary, look back at the original source: *Did you capture the original concepts and integrate your own interpretation into your writing?*

Even when you write about someone's ideas in your own words, you still need to cite the original source. Let us take a look at some examples. First, compare the original writing with each of the two samples. As you examine each example, determine if the writer did an accurate job of *paraphrasing* or *summarizing*:

Original text: "Gambrill's (2003) research indicates many gaps exist in the literature. Therefore, social workers must be actively involved in conducting and publishing research to fulfill their ethical obligation" (Young, 2014, p. 55).

Example 1: Gambrill's (2003) research ***shows that there*** are many gaps in the literature. Social workers ***need to engage in*** conducting and publishing research to fulfill their ethical obligation (Young, 2014).

Example 2: Social workers inform their practice with research. Unfortunately, there are many unanswered research questions (Gambrill, 2003). Through additional research, social workers are more likely to engage in effective and competent practice, an ethical requirement of the profession.

Discussion: Sample 1 is not an accurate paraphrase because the author did not write it in his or her own words, but substituted only a few words. Sample 2, on the other hand, is an accurate summary. *Can you see the difference?*

Here is another example:

Original Text: "Synthesis is associated with creating, innovating, and inventing. Synthesis involves putting together elements or parts to form a whole, arranging or combining pieces, parts, and elements to develop a pattern or structure that was not clearly there before" (Tamburro, 2014, p. 80).

Example: To synthesize is to create, innovate, and invent. Synthesizing involves putting together parts to develop a pattern (Tamburro, 2014).

Is the above example paraphrasing? Has this writer demonstrated an understanding of the concept?

Activity 2.5

Summarizing and Paraphrasing

Instructions: Read the original text below and then summarize it.

Original text: When social workers write case notes, they must be clear, accurate, and concise because it becomes a permanent record. Oral and written communication are essential professional social work skills.

Write your summary below:

_____

_____

_____

_____

Revising Sentences

An important skill in revising is presenting the same information in different ways and understanding how readers might be affected by the differences.

To start, let go of the idea that there is "one right way" to state information. Most ideas can be stated in many different ways, each having a slightly different effect on the reader. It is a matter of syntax and choice.

Composing is the most difficult part of the writing process. As you edit and revise, do not become attached to specific sentences. To loosen up your revising skills, let us examine how to portray the same information in different ways. The following sentences present the same information:

> We would like to convey our appreciation for your assistance with the grant.
>
> Thank you for helping us with the grant.
>
> We appreciate your help with the grant.
>
> Your help with the grant was valuable, and we appreciate it.
>
> The valuable assistance you gave us with the grant is appreciated.
>
> Please accept our appreciation for your assistance with the grant.

With which of the above sentences sounds most effective to you? Why did you choose that sentence?

Here's another example:

> Your grant proposal has been received within the deadline and is being reviewed by our committee.
>
> Thank you for sending your grant proposal; when final decisions are made, you will hear from us.
>
> Our committee is reviewing your grant proposal, and you will hear the results of their decision by May 1.
>
> Your grant proposal is being considered for funding; we will contact you with our decision by May 1.

Now work on Activity 2.6 to get some practice revising sentences.

Activity 2.6

Revising Sentences

Instructions: Writers are sometimes attached to the idea that there is "one right way" to say something. However, most ideas can be expressed in a multitude of ways. To loosen up your revising skills, develop three or four versions of each sentence below. Feel free to expand on the idea by adding appreciation or an apology, if needed.

Analyze the changes and consider how the changes affect the tone. Finally, which sentence among your revisions expresses the original idea best?

1. An incorrect report was accidentally sent to you last week by our agency.

2. Your position for a case worker is of interest to me.

3. George did not respond to my invitation about joining our committee.

Note: See page 210 for the key to this activity.

Workshop Assignments

Application 2.1

Editing E-Mail

Instructions: Select an e-mail message that you have written to a professor and edit the message by applying the principles that you learned in this workshop.

1. Put the original message and the revision in one Word file, which you will submit to your professor as an attachment to a process message.

2. In the process message to your professor, analyze the changes that you made in the revision and discuss what you learned.

Application 2.2

Editing Paragraphs

Instructions: Select a paper that you have previously written. Identify 2 or 3 paragraphs to revise. As you edit and revise your writing, also *analyze the kinds of changes you are making*: which principles are you applying to improve the quality and flow of your writing?

This assignment consists of the following parts:

1. Original Writing
2. Revision
3. Analysis
4. Process Message

- *For the revision,* use **tracking**.

    o   Under the **Review** tab in your Word toolbar, click on **Track Changes** to show the markup for changes you are making. (In Word 2013 you may need to click the bar on the left of your edits to show the markup.)

    o   Save 2 copies of your revision: one with tracking on, and one with tracking off.

- *In the analysis*, discuss the changes you made and principles that you applied.

- Send your professor this assignment as an attachment to a *process message* in which you discuss what you learned.

  o Put the original and two revisions (one with tracking on and one with tracking off) in one Word document.

Application 2.3
E-Mail Etiquette: Netiquette

Instructions: Online writing is an element of most classes and almost all jobs. To understand what might be expected from you in this class and on the job, read "Process Messages," pages xi – xii, and "Best Practices for E-Communication," pages 195 – 202. Also feel free to research netiquette online.

What did you learn about online writing?

1. How should you to structure an e-mail message?

2. What are 5 basic rules of netiquette that you will apply?

Pre-Work for Workshop 3
Conjunctions as Signals

Instructions: In Workshop 3, you learn that *conjunctions function as signals* for commas and semicolons. In *The Writer's Handbook: A Guide for Social Workers*, read pages 164 through 167. Answer each question below, listing each type of conjunction:

What role do *coordinating conjunctions* play in a sentence? (List a few.)

What role do *subordinating conjunctions* play? (List a few of the most common.)

What role do *adverbial conjunctions* play? (List a few of the most common.)

Notes

3

Punctuate for Purpose, *Not* Pauses

Oscar Wilde illustrated the confusion surrounding commas and pauses perfectly when he said, "I have spent most of the day putting in a comma and the rest of the day taking it out." If you have had extensive experience with punctuation and still feel unsure about using commas and semicolons correctly, you are not alone.

In fact, placing commas correctly may seem confusing because you base your decisions on *guesses* rather than *principles*. In this workshop, you learn valid reasons for placing commas. Thus, from this point on, if you do not know *why* you are putting a comma in, do *not* use one.

When in doubt, leave the comma out.

If you cannot state the comma rule that applies, you may be using the comma incorrectly. To enhance what you learn, identify the *sentence core* of each of the practice sentences. If you need a review of the sentence core, see Chapter 8, "Dynamic Sentences," in *The Writer's Handbook: A Guide for Social Workers* (2014).

Reviewing comma use has a big payoff: as you apply commas according to a system that works, you eliminate sentence fragments, run-on sentences, and comma splices. As you take control of structure, you also become more confident with your writing.

The Plan

1. Take the **pretest** on page 38.
2. Answer the questions in the **Workshop Inventory** on page 39.
3. Review **Part 1: Comma Rules.**
4. Complete **Activity 3.1: Commas** on page 47.
5. Review **Part 2: Semicolon Rules**.
6. Complete **Activity 3.2: Commas and Semicolons** on page 51.
7. Take the **posttest** on page 52; compare pretest and posttest results.
8. To further refine your skills, complete the exercises in Chapter 10, "Comma Rules" and Chapter 11, "Semicolon Rules" in *The Writer's Handbook: A Guide for Social Workers* (2014).

Pretest

Instructions: Insert commas and semicolons in the following sentences.

1. If you are unable to attend the meeting find a replacement immediately.

2. Should Bob Jesse and Marlene discuss these issues with you?

3. As soon as we receive your application we will process your account.

4. Your new checks were shipped last month therefore you should have received them by now.

5. Will you be attending the seminar in Dallas Texas on December 15 2015?

6. Fortunately my manager values my efforts and believes in my ability to do quality work.

7. Mr. Adams when you have time please review this contract for me.

8. We received his portfolio on May 15 and we promptly developed a new strategy.

9. Carrie brought her report to the meeting however it was not complete.

10. Mr. Jensen sent a letter to my supervisor the letter was complimentary.

11. The merger however required that each corporation learn to trust the other.

12. Thank you Donald for supporting our quality assurance efforts.

13. I am not sure about the costs but I recommend that we consider this proposal.

14. We received the contract yesterday however we have not yet reviewed it.

15. Mr. Wells will arrive on Wednesday November 18 as he stated in his letter.

Note: See page 211 for the key to this pretest.

Workshop 3 Inventory

Instructions: Read and answer the questions below.

1. Commas are placed in sentences based on pauses.   T/F

2. A sentence has a _____ and a _____ and expresses a complete thought.

3. A sentence is   a) a dependent clause, or b) an independent clause.

4. Which of the following is a dependent clause:

    a. Your friend arrived.

    b. When your friend arrived.

    c. After your friend arrived, we worked on the project.

5. In English, the subject of a sentence generally precedes the verb.   T/F

6. Which of the following is not a subordinating conjunction:

    a. when   c. since

    b. after   d. however

7. Which of the following is not an adverbial conjunction:

    a. therefore   c. if

    b. for example   d. consequently

8. If a subordinating conjunction such as *if*, *when*, or *although* is placed at the beginning of an independent clause, the clause will become dependent.   T/F

9. Conjunctions signal where to place commas in a sentence.   T/F

10. One comma can be correctly placed between the subject and verb of a sentence.   T/F

11. The subject and verb are the core of a sentence.   T/F

12. Commas are placed based on pauses.   T/F

Note: See page 212 for the key to this inventory.

PART 1: COMMA RULES

As you go through the following 12 comma rules, underline the verb of each example twice and the subject one time. Also, take the time to review conjunctions carefully (see page 41), as they play an intricate role in placing punctuation correctly.

Rule 1: The Sentence Core Rules (SCR)

Do not separate a subject and verb with only one comma.

Incorrect: Mr. Jones, asked that the meeting begin on time.

Corrected: Mr. Jones asked that the meeting begin on time.

As you will see, setting off information with a pair of commas is acceptable.

- When identifying subjects and verbs, identify the verb first and then work backward in the sentence to identify the grammatical subject.
- Underline main verbs two times simple subjects one time.

Rule 2: Conjunction (CONJ)

Use a comma to separate independent clauses when they are joined by a coordinating conjunction (and, but, or, for, nor, so, yet).

Mary would like to go to the meeting, but she has a conflict.

FINDING VERBS AND SUBJECTS

1. When identifying subjects and verbs, identify the verb first and then work backward in the sentence to identify the grammatical subject.

2. Remember to consider "you understood" or an "implied you" as the subject when the grammatical subject is not easily identified. You can represent *you understood* as follows: (you).

   For example: (You) Please take a seat.

3. Also remember to consider "I understood" as an implied subject.

   For example: (I) Thank you.

4. The base form of a verb is known as an *infinitive.* Infinitives do not transfer action and do not function as the verb in a sentence.

CONJUNCTIONS AS COMMA SIGNALS

Conjunctions indicate where to put a comma or semicolon—learn the three types to ensure that you punctuate correctly.

A. **COORDINATIING CONJUNCTIONS** connect independent clauses or items in a series. When needed, put a comma *before* a coordinating conjunction, not after.

> and   but   or   for   nor   so   yet

B. **SUBORDINATING CONJUNCTIONS** show relationships by introducing dependent clauses and phrases.

as	after	since	unless
because	although	until	whereas
if	even though	while	as soon as
when	though	so that	before

C. **ADVERBIAL CONJUNCTIONS** introduce or interrupt independent clauses. Adverbial conjunctions build bridges, helping the reader infer the writer's intent.

> however, in addition, moreover, furthermore, what is more, consequently, therefore, thus, accordingly, in any event, in conclusion, in short, in summary, as usual, indeed, unfortunately, nevertheless, for example, in general, usually, of course, *and so on.*

Rule 3: Introductory (INTRO)

Place a comma after a word (an adverbial conjunction), phrase, or dependent clause that introduces a main clause.

> **Furthermore**, their <u>discount</u> <u>reduced</u> our cost.
>
> **After the meeting**, George offered to chair the committee.
>
> **When your client arrived**, you both began working on the project.

- Common **adverbial conjunctions** include *however, therefore, for example,* and *thus.*
- Common **subordinating conjunctions** include *although, because, if, as, as soon as, before, since,* and *so that.*

In the above examples, did you underline each verb twice and its subject once?

Rule 4: Nonrestrictive (NR)

Use commas to set off nonrestrictive explanations that are nonessential to the meaning of the sentence.

Nonessential information often comes in the form of "who" or "which" clauses.

A. Phyllis Smith and Jane Adams, who ran for office last year, attended the meeting.
B. The two women who ran for office last year attended the meeting.

Rule 5: Parenthetical (PAR)

Use commas to set off a word or phrase that interrupts an independent clause.

A. Our team will, *however*, need more time to complete the report.
B. The proposal is due, *I believe*, next Friday by 5 p.m.

Rule 6: Direct Address (DA)

Use commas to set off the name or title of a person addressed directly.

A. Our agency, *Mrs. Roberts*, appreciates your support.
B. *Mr. Adams*, our mission supports your cause.
C. Please, *sir*, take a seat in the waiting room.

When identifying the subject in sentence C above, remember that a subject and verb cannot be separated by only one comma.

Rule 7: Appositive (AP)

Use commas to set off words or phrases that describe or identify a preceding noun or pronoun.

A. Charles, my associate, will join us at 8 o'clock.
B. The president, Mr. Sims, prefers that meetings begin on time.

Rule 8: Addresses and Dates (A/D)

Use commas to set off addresses and dates.

A. John listed January 5, 2010, as his start date.
B. She has lived in Springfield, Illinois, for the past six years.
C. Boston, Massachusetts, is a great city for a conference.

Rule 9: Series (SER)

Use *a comma to separate three or more items in a series.*

A. George would like potatoes, peas, and carrots for dinner.
B. The estate was left to George, Alice, Bob, and Rose.

- For grammatical correctness, the comma before *and* in a series is optional; however, putting in the comma makes the meaning clearer.
- For legal documents, it is important that a comma be placed before *and* so that parties are recognized as separate entitles.

   (Note: This comma rule supports the use of the "Oxford comma," which is much debated. It's called the Oxford comma because Oxford University takes a stand that a comma should be placed before "and" in a series.)

Rule 10: Word Omitted (WO)

Use a comma for the omission of a word or words that play a structural role in sentences.

This type of comma occurs infrequently. Most of the time, the word that has been omitted is either *that* or *and*.

   The problem is *that* the current situation is quite grim.

   The problem is, the current situation is quite grim.

   Mr. Adams presented the long *and* boring report to the board.

   Mr. Adams presented the long, boring report to the board.

Rule 11: Direct Quotation (DQ)

Use commas to set off direct quotations within a sentence.

A direct quotation is a person's exact words. In comparison, an indirect quotation does not give a speaker's exact words and would *not* be set off with commas.

Direct Quotation: Gabrielle said, "I have a 9 o'clock appointment," and then left the meeting abruptly.

Indirect Quotation: Gabrielle said that she had a 9 o'clock appointment and then left the meeting abruptly.

Direct Quotation: Dr. Gorman asked, "Is the environment experiencing global warming at a faster rate than predicted?"

Indirect Quotation: Dr. Gorman asked whether the environment is experiencing global warming at a faster rate than predicted.

An exception to this rule relates to short quotations: a short quotation built into the flow of a sentence does not need to be set off with commas.

Short Quotations: Marian shouted "Help!" as she ran.

     My boss told me "Meet the deadline at all costs."

     The advice "Give the project your best this time" sounded patronizing rather than encouraging.

With direct quotations, whether set off with commas or blending with the flow of the sentence, capitalize the first word of the quotation.

Using punctuation with quotation marks can be confusing; therefore, consistently apply the following guidelines, which adhere to *closed punctuation style.*

Punctuation placement with quotation marks:
- Place commas and periods on the *inside* of quotation marks.
- Place semicolons and colons on the *outside* of quotation marks.
- Place exclamation marks and question marks based on meaning: these marks can go on the *inside* or *outside* of quotation marks.

Regardless of where you place a punctuation mark, *never* double punctuate at the end of a sentence.

Rule 12: Contrasting Expression or Afterthought (CEA)

Use a comma to separate a contrasting expression or afterthought.

A contrasting expression or afterthought adds an interesting twist to writing style. The expression at the end of the sentence certainly gets the reader's attention, for example:

A. Go ahead and try to quit smoking, if you can.
B. I asked for the information so that I could help Bill find employment, not find a job for him.
C. His cousin John, not his brother Buddy, has become homeless.

In fact, omitting the CEA comma is not a serious error; however, using the CEA comma makes your comments stand out and gives your writing a conversational flow.

Next Steps

Now that you have reviewed all 12 basic comma rules, complete Activity 3.1 on page 47. To develop an understanding of structure, following the instructions precisely by doing the following:

1. Underline the main verb of each independent clause.
2. Underline the grammatical subject.
3. Identify the reason or rule for the comma, for example, *is it a comma INTRO? . . . a comma CONJ? . . . a comma DA? . . .* and so on.

Though you may not fully understand the rationale right now, you will be achieving multiple outcomes. For example, by underlining the verb and its subject, you are gaining control of the sentence core—the most important unit of grammar and editing.

As you develop a deeper understanding of the sentence core, you also develop more proficiency in the following:

- Turning fragments into complete sentences.
- Correcting run-on sentences.
- Tuning in to correct subject-verb agreement.
- Using subjective and objective pronouns correctly.

After you complete Activity 3.1, go on to semicolons and complete Activity 3.2 in the same manner. *Work with a partner and have fun!*

Comma Rules

Rule 1: The Sentence Core Rules (SCR)
Do not separate a subject and verb with only one comma.

Rule 2: Conjunction (CONJ)
*Use a comma to separate two independent clauses
when they are joined by a coordinating conjunction
(and, but, or, nor, for, so, yet).*

Rule 3: Series (SER)
Use a comma to separate three or more items in a series.

Rule 4: Introductory (INTRO)
*Place a comma after a word, phrase, or dependent clause
that introduces an independent clause.*

Rule 5: Nonrestrictive (NR)
Use commas to set off nonessential (nonrestrictive) words and phrases.

Rule 6: Parenthetical (PAR)
Use commas to set off a word or expression that interrupts the flow of a sentence.

Rule 7: Direct Address (DA)
Use commas to set off the name or title of a person addressed directly.

Rule 8: Appositive (AP)
Use commas to set off the restatement of a noun or pronoun.

Rule 9: Addresses and Dates (AD)
Use commas to set off the parts of addresses and dates.

Rule 10: Word Omitted (WO)
Use a comma for the omission of a word or words that play a structural role in a sentence.

Rule 11: Direct Quotation (DQ)
Use commas to set off direct quotations within a sentence.

Rule 12: Contrasting Expression or Afterthought (CEA)
Use a comma to separate a contrasting expression or afterthought.

REVIEW TIP

COORDINATING CONJUNCTIONS
connect equal grammatical parts:

and but or for nor so yet

SUBORDINATING CONJUNCTIONS
introduce dependent clauses and
phrases: *after, since, unless, because,
while, until, before, although, if, so that,
when, as soon as, though, even
though,* and so on.

ADVERBIAL CONJUNCTIONS
introduce or interrupt independent
clauses: *however, therefore, for
example, consequently, as a result,
though, thus, fortunately, in addition,
in short, in general, of course, in
summary,* and so on.

Activity 3.1

Comma Practice

Instructions: Correct the sentences below for the following types of comma use:

Introductory (INTRO)   **Appositive (AP)**

Direct Address (DA)   **Address/Date (AD)**

1. Underline the verb in each sentence twice and the subject once. *Note*: If you cannot locate the subject, it may be "you understood."
2. Identify the reason (INTRO, AP, or DA) for using each comma.

Example: As the <u>doctor</u> <u>ordered</u>, <u>I</u> <u>stayed</u> in bed all week. INTRO

1. Before he entered the building the young man checked the address.

2. If you would like the agency to process your request leave your number and a time you can be reached.

3. George can I count on your assistance?

4. Mr. Jones the building manager keeps all of the leases.

5. So that you are able to focus on your meeting we will hold all calls and interruptions.

6. After the chairperson made the announcement the group was in chaos.

7. In general we do not include that information on our Web site.

8. Ms. Whitehead please e-mail me the information if that is convenient.

9. Even though you do not like the referral it is our only option.

10. Cathy when will you inform your task group?

11. Please speak to Louise our assistant if I am not in the office.

12. Although it is important to be on time it is also important to be prepared.

13. Until the director arrives we cannot begin the meeting.

14. She went to visit her sister in Detroit Michigan last year sometime.

15. He lists his start date as Friday September 19 2007.

Note: See page 212 for the key to this activity.

PART 2: SEMICOLON RULES

Do you have an aversion to using semicolons? Many people avoid semicolons; and in doing so, they put commas in their place. By using a comma where a semicolon belongs, a writer is creating a serious grammatical error.

Consider the following points about semicolons:

- As a general rule, *you can use a semicolon where you could use a period.*

- Semicolons can be used when one or both sentences are short and closely related in meaning.

- Sentences can be punctuated correctly in more than one way.

1. Semicolon No Conjunction (NC)

Use a semicolon to separate two independent clauses that are joined without a conjunction. This rule is sometimes referred to as "semicolon in place of period."

> They <u>invited</u> me to join the board; <u>I decided</u> that I would.

Also correct:

> They invited me to join the board, *and* I decided that I would. (CONJ)
> They invited me to join the board. I decided that I would.

2. Semicolon Transition (TRANS)

Place a semicolon before and a comma after adverbial conjunctions (such as however, therefore, consequently, *and* nevertheless) *when they act as transitions between independent clauses.*

> Jane invited Tim to the meeting; however, he was not able to attend.

Also correct:

> Jane invited Tim to the meeting. Tim, however, was not able to attend.
> Jane invited Time to the meeting, but he was not able to attend.

3. Semicolon Because of Comma (BC)

When a clause needs major and minor separations, use semicolons for major breaks and commas for minor breaks.

Apply this rule when listing a series of city and state names, for example:

Semicolon BC: Joni will travel to conferences in Dallas, Texas; Buffalo, New York; and Boston, Massachusetts.

Since the state names need commas around them, reading the above sentence without semicolons would be confusing:

Incorrect: Joni will travel to conferences in Dallas, Texas, Buffalo, New York, and Boston, Massachusetts.

Also apply this rule when listing a series of names and titles:

Semicolon BC: The committee members are Jeremy Smith, director; Marjorie Lou Kirk, office manager; Carson Michaels, accountant; and Mallory Willowbrook, representative for case workers.

Here is a more complicated example that has major and minor clauses:

Semicolon BC: Millicent asked for a raise; and since she was a new employee, I deferred to Jackson's opinion.

Semicolon BC: Dr. Jones suggested the procedure; but I was unable to help, so he asked Dr. Cordes.

This semicolon rule differs from the other two rules because it does not involve a *full stop*; in other words, this rule does not follow the "semicolon in place of period" guideline.

The Comma Versus the Semicolon

At times, commas and semicolons provide similar functions. For example, comma conjunction (CONJ) and semicolon no conjunction (NC) can each be used when a sentence consists of two independent clauses:

Cate <u>works</u> in the Chicago office, and <u>she</u> <u>purchases</u> supplies each Monday. (CONJ)
Cate <u>works</u> in the Chicago office; <u>she</u> <u>purchases</u> supplies each Monday. (NC)

However, neither a comma nor a semicolon would be used if the sentence had a compound verb:

Correct: Cate <u>works</u> in the Chicago office and <u>purchases</u> supplies each Monday.

Incorrect: Cate <u>works</u> in the Chicago office**,** and <u>purchases</u> supplies each Monday.

Comma parenthetical (PAR) and semicolon transition (TRANS) are sometimes confused, **for example:**

Cate <u>works</u> in the Chicago office; however, <u>she</u> <u>does</u> not <u>purchase</u> supplies. (NC)
Cate, however, does not <u>purchase</u> supplies. (PAR)

Can you see how the incorrect punctuation in the following are confused with the semicolon transition (TRANS) and the comma parenthetical (PAR):

Incorrect: Cate <u>works</u> in the office**,** however**,** <u>she</u> <u>does</u> not <u>purchase</u> supplies.

Incorrect: <u>Cate</u>**;** however**,** <u>does</u> not <u>purchase</u> supplies.

Semicolon Rules

1. **Semicolon No Conjunction (NC)**

   Use a semicolon to separate two independent clauses that are joined without a conjunction.

2. **Semicolon Transition (TRANS)**

   Use a semicolon before and a comma after an adverbial conjunction that bridges two independent clauses.

3. **Semicolon Because of Comma (BC)**

   When a clause needs major and minor separations, use semicolons for major breaks and commas for minor breaks.

Activity 3.2

Commas and Semicolons

Instructions: Correct the sentences below for the following comma and semicolon use:

Comma Conjunction (CONJ)   **Semicolon No Conjunction (NC)**

Comma Parenthetical (PAR)   **Semicolon Transition (TRANS)**

1. Underline the verb in each main clause twice and its subject once. *Note:* If you cannot locate the subject, it may be "you understood."
2. Identify the reason (listed above) for using each comma and semicolon.

Incorrect: Ty went to the meeting however Lee stayed to meet with a client.

Corrected: Ty <u>went</u> to the meeting; however, <u>Lee</u> <u>stayed</u> to meet with a client. TRANS

1. George wanted to go to the conference but he had a previous commitment.
2. He had told her about the meeting she refused to go.
3. We therefore are sending the material by Federal Express.
4. Mr. Adams gave the statistics but there were many people who did not believe him.
5. The issue was resolved once we understood the problem this was a great relief.
6. Alexander went to school Martin preferred to skip school.
7. They told us the information too late so we were not able to attend.
8. The new printer does not work as effectively as the old one but it is ours now.
9. Mary wants to go to the seminar however her supervisor will not approve the expenses.
10. Susan did well on the proposal unfortunately she was not in the meeting to receive feedback.
11. Mr. Jones never arrives on time for example he arrived ten minutes late to our last meeting.
12. The contract states however that extended family members can attend sessions.
13. Please send the information to George Schmidt he expected it earlier this week.
14. We therefore look forward to seeing you on Friday please call if your schedule changes.
15. Bill is a good candidate for that job he received a recommendation from his manager.
16. The storm knocked out the power consequently the family could not contact us.

Note: See page 213 for the key to this activity.

Posttest

Instructions: Insert commas and semicolons in the following sentences.

1. We received his letter on May 15 2014 explaining his concerns.

2. Mr. Harris will be here on Tuesday September 18 as stated in the memo.

3. When you have finished Mr. Harkness please review this contract for me.

4. We received your application yesterday however we have not yet had a chance to review it.

5. Unfortunately my manager does not value my work as much as she should.

6. I am not sure about the benefits but I wonder if this approach would be useful.

7. Will you be attending the conference in Springfield Illinois on November 10 2016?

8. Thank you Ms. Vandergelt for supporting our efforts.

9. Your report was sent on Tuesday therefore you should have received it by now.

10. The proposal however required that each agency learn to trust the other.

11. As soon as we receive these documents we will send you the verification.

12. Ms. Smith sent a letter to my supervisor the letter was very complimentary.

13. Would you like for Mark Jodie and Arlene to bring up these issues with you?

14. Della brought her calendar to the meeting but I forgot mine.

15. If you are unable to attend the conference inform your supervisor immediately.

Note: See page 213 for the key to this posttest.

For additional practice, go to **www.thewriterstoolkit.com**. Click on the menu at the top left side of the page for exercises on punctuation as well as other topics.

Notes

4

Keep Verbs Active

The hub of every sentence is its verb, and the way writers use verbs helps determine the quality of their writing.

When a writer uses verbs incorrectly, each mistake detracts from the credibility of the writing and, at times, the writer. When writers use the passive voice unnecessarily and excessively, their writing style becomes tedious and unfriendly to readers. This chapter addresses those issues and is broken into two parts:

- **Part 1: Tense and Mood**, which focuses on writing correctly.

- **Part 2: Active Voice**, which focuses on developing an effective writing style.

Start by assessing your skill profile so that you identify the kinds of mistakes that you make. Errors come in patterns; so when you correct one type of error, you improve the quality of your writing significantly. After covering principles on correct usage, you cover principles to improve your writing style, such as active voice.

The Plan

1. Take the **pretest** on page 56.

2. Complete **Workshop 4 Inventory** on page 56.

3. Review **Part 1: Verbs—Tense and Mood**, pages 57 – 61.

4. Complete the **Irregular Verb Inventory**, page 58.

5. Complete Activity 4.1 on page 62 and Activities 4.2, 4.3, and 4.4 on page 63.

6. Review **Part 2: Active Voice**, page 64; complete Activity 4.5, Active Voice, page 65.

7. Review **Nominalization**, page 66 and complete Activity 4.6, Nominalization, page 67.

8. Take the **posttest** on page 68; compare pretest and posttest results.

9. *For additional explanation and practice*, complete all exercises in Chapter 12, "Verbs," Chapter 15, "Active Voice," and Chapter 16, "Parallel Structure" in *The Writer's Handbook: A Guide for Social Workers* (2014).

Pretest

Instructions: Identify and correct the errors in the following sentences.

1. After Bob had quietly spoke his answer, everyone agreed.
2. A social worker said that you are unhappy about our service.
3. The pamphlet include the information you are looking for.
4. If I was you, I would support Tim in his decision.
5. Our acquisition budget is froze until the fourth quarter.
6. Margarite commend Albert for the job he does every day.
7. I would've went to the meeting opening if I had been invited.
8. Austin had gave the report to the committee.
9. You should of spoke to their family while the incident was still fresh.
10. Every member of the committee attend the conference last June.

Workshop 4 Inventory

Instructions: Read and answer the questions below.

1. The subject and verb together form the core of a sentence.   T/F
2. All verbs have both a past tense form and a past participle form.   T/F
3. A helper verb (such as *is*, *has*, or *do*) must be used with a past participle form.   T/F
4. The verb in a sentence determines its grammatical subject.   T/F
5. For irregular verbs, add *ed* to form both the past tense and past participle.   T/F
6. The base form of a verb is called an infinitive.   T/F
7. All third person singular verbs in English end in *s*.   T/F
8. In the active voice, the *subject*, *verb*, and *object* perform their prescribed grammatical functions.   T/F
9. A *nominalization* is a noun that originated as a verb.   T/F
10. The subjunctive mood expresses possibility, not fact.   T/F

Note: See page 214 for the key to the pretest and inventory above.

PART 1: VERBS—TENSE AND MOOD

Based on the way past tense is formed, verbs are broken down into two broad categories: *regular verbs* and *irregular verbs*. In addition to past time, writers make errors using the −s form, or third person singular.

Irregular Verbs in Past Time

- When using the past participle of an irregular verb, you *must* use a helper.
- When using the past form of an irregular verb, you *cannot* use a helper.

Here are a few irregular verbs with helper verbs that were randomly chosen.

Base	Past	Past Participle
do	did	(have) done
go	went	(is) gone
see	saw	(are) seen
speak	spoke	(was) spoken
write	wrote	(were) written

For **irregular verbs**, here are the **two most common errors**:

1. Using an irregular past form with a helper.

   Examples: Mary *has wrote* the report. (correction: *has written*)
   The budget *is froze* until next year. (correction: *is frozen*)
   The director *has spoke* about that problem. (correction: *has spoken*)

2. Using an irregular past participle without a helper.

   Examples: Margaret *seen* Bob at the conference. (correction: *saw*)
   They *done* the work last week. (correction: *did*)
   Alice *gone* to the store late last evening. (correction: *went*)

Irregular Verb Inventory

Instructions: Fill in the past tense and past participle forms below. Use a helper verb, such as to be (is, are, was, were) or to have (*has, have,* or *had*) with each past participle.

Base Form	Past Tense	Past Participle
arise	arose	*have* arisen
become	became	*has* become
break	broke	*was* broken
bring	_____	_____
buy	_____	_____
choose	_____	_____
do	_____	_____
drink	_____	_____
drive	_____	_____
eat	_____	_____
fly	_____	_____
forget	_____	_____
freeze	_____	_____
get	_____	_____
forget	_____	_____
go	_____	_____
know	_____	_____
lend	_____	_____
prove	_____	_____
say	_____	_____
see	_____	_____
set	_____	_____
sink	_____	_____
sit	_____	_____
show	_____	_____
speak	_____	_____
stand	_____	_____
take	_____	_____
throw	_____	_____
write	_____	_____

Note: See page 69 for the key to the Irregular Verb Inventory.

Regular Verbs in Past Time

The vast majority of verbs are regular, which means that the past tense and past participle forms are both created by adding –ed to the base form, for example:

Base	Past Tense	Past Participle
walk	walked	*have* walked
comment	commented	*had* commented
argue	argued	*have* argued

Here are some examples of how errors are made with past tense verbs in Edited English:

Incorrect:	We *walk* to the professor's office yesterday after class.
Corrected:	We *walked* to the professor's office yesterday after class.
Incorrect:	The committee *argue* all afternoon.
Corrected:	The committee *argued* all afternoon.

Third Person Singular: The —S Form

In Edited English, all third person singular verbs in simple present tense end in an *s*. By referring to third person singular verbs as the –*s* form, you remain aware of their unique spelling.

Here are some examples:

Incorrect:	Bob **don't** give the information to anyone.
Corrected:	Bob **does not** (doesn't) give the information to anyone.
Incorrect:	Martha **have** the right attitude about her job.
Corrected:	Martha **has** the right attitude about her job.

Verb Tense and Consistency

Within the same sentence and paragraph, keep verbs in a consistent tense (unless you give the reader a cue that you are changing time). This error is sometimes difficult to find: Verbs may be conjugated correctly, but their inconsistent use creates the problem.

Incorrect: We *finished* the meeting early because we *are going* to another site.

Revised: We *finished* the meeting early because we *were going* to another site.

Subjunctive Mood

Mood is a grammatical term used to describe a writer's attitude toward a subject as it is expressed by the form of the verb. Most people do not have a problem with the indicative or imperative moods. If an error is to be made, it is with the subjunctive mood.

The subjunctive mood expresses improbability. When a statement conveys a *wish* or a *possibility*, it should be made in the subjunctive mood. The subjunctive mood is also used with certain requests, demands, recommendations, and set phrases.

- For the **past subjunctive**, *to be* is always expressed as *were*.
  (As in, "if I *were* you . . .")

- For the **present subjunctive**, the verb is expressed in the **infinitive** form.
  (As in, *it is important that she go to the meeting.*)

Statements Following "Wish" or "If"

If something is a *wish*, it means it is not a statement of fact; thus, statements following "wish" should be made in the subjunctive mood. In a subjunctive statement, the verb **"to be"** will always be represented as **"were."**

Incorrect:	Revised:
I *wish* I **was** able to be there.	I *wish* I **were** able to be there.
She *wishes* he **was** able to attend.	She *wishes* he **were** able to attend.
They *wish* it **was** true.	They *wish* it **were** true.

When a sentence begins with the word "if," very often the statement that follows is not a fact, but a *condition*. Those statements should also be made in the subjunctive mood.

Incorrect: If he *was* more positive, it would seem easier.

If she *was* more mature, she would understand their decision.

If I *was* you, I would go to the seminar.

Corrected: If he *were* more positive, it would seem easier.

If she *were* more mature, she would understand their decision.

If I *were* you, I would go to the seminar.

Present Subjunctive

The present subjunctive is expressed by the infinitive form of the verb, regardless of the person or number of the subject. The present subjunctive occurs in *that clauses* after verbs expressing wishes, commands, requests, or recommendations.

The manager said that* it is imperative you be on time.

It is essential (that) he take you to the meeting.

He suggested (that) the committee be disbanded.

Bob requested (that) Sarah repeat her answer.

*The word "that" is a function word and is implied even when it is removed from a sentence. However, do not remove the word "that" from a statement when the words "said" or "reported" precede it. Otherwise, a paraphrase might be misinterpreted as a quote; for example:

Unclear: Martha said Bob will chair the meeting

Clear: Martha said that Bob will chair the meeting.
Clear: Martha said, "Bob will chair the meeting."

Activity 4.1

Tense, Agreement, Consistency, and Mood

Instructions: Choose the correct form of the verb (or adverb); make corrections where needed.

1. We had finally (did, done) our part of the work.
2. He should not have (went, gone) to the office on Friday.
3. She (don't, doesn't) give that information to no one.
4. She had (spoke, spoken) (eloquent, eloquently) at the conference.
5. He (loaned, lent) me the material for the meeting.
6. You should have (wrote, written, writen) to the office first.
7. The phone must have (rang, rung) 20 times before they answered.
8. I should (of, have) (brang, brung, brought) another copy.
9. Who has (drunk, drank) the last glass of juice?
10. We were (near, nearly) (froze, frozen) when they arrived.
11. She should have easily (saw, seen) the error in the report.
12. We ate (quick, quickly) because we (are, were) going to the meeting.
13. They were (took, taken) by surprise.
14. She (has, have) (chose, chosen) the most beautiful graphic.
15. (May, Can) I assist you with the project?
16. They would have (swam, swum) if they had more time.
17. My heart (sunk, sank) when she gave the news.
18. The budget is (froze, frozen) until next quarter.
19. Try (and, to) drive more careful.
20. Ever since I (got, have) a new manager, I always (got, have) too much work.
21. She felt bad because he (is, was) not available to assist us.
22. That was the most (silliest, silly) decision he ever made.
23. Bob's supervisor was concerned that he (is, was) not able to complete the project.
24. He felt (bad, badly) about the situation and (wants, wanted) to help.
25. She advised him to drive (safe, safely) because his new car (runs, ran) (bad, badly).
26. If I (was, were) you, I would (of, have) gone to the meeting.
27. I wish she (was, were) my client.
28. If Tom (was, were) your manager, (will, would) you go to the conference?

Note: See page 215 for the key to this activity.

Activity 4.2

Subjunctive Mood

Instructions: Circle the correct form of the verb for the subjunctive mood.

1. The supervisor requested that Mike (*invite, invites*) the new manager to the meeting.
2. John wishes he (*was, were*) in charge of the new agency.
3. If Lester (*was, were*) on your team, would you support him?
4. It is imperative that she (*complete, completes*) the proposal.
5. If Tiffany (*was, were*) your manager, (*would, will*) you attend the conference?

Activity 4.3

Consistent Tense

Instructions: Correct the following for errors in tense.

had

Example: I called the director yesterday because I ~~have~~ an all-day meeting today.

1. My manager says we should have gotten the report finished sooner.
2. John gave me the report today because he wants to take Friday as a vacation day.
3. Five computer terminals were broken, so the manager is requesting all new ones.
4. My advisor informs me of class openings, but I signed up for the wrong ones.
5. The program analysis was difficult to complete, and our team requires more time.
6. The inscription on the plaque was blurry and needs to be corrected.

Activity 4.4

Past Tense

Instructions: Correct the following for errors in past tense.

Incorrect: My assistant help me with the project.

Corrected: My assistant *helped* me with the project.

1. Bob finally indicate that the information was wrong.
2. The dean encourage me to apply for graduate school.
3. My interview result in a job offer at another company.
4. Ms. Fielding told me that their agency merge with a larger one last year.
5. Have you plan for the interview?

Note: See page 216 for the keys to the above activities.

PART 2: ACTIVE VOICE

The active voice is easier to understand than the passive voice—the active voice is direct and uses fewer words. More importantly, in the active voice, the **subject**, **verb**, and **object** perform their prescribed grammatical functions. Let's start with a passive sentence:

Passive: The papers were sent to Sue by Bob.

First, identify the main verb, which is *sent*. Next, identify *who performed the action of the verb*. So ask yourself, *who* sent the papers?

Active: Bob *sent* the papers (to Sue).

Here are the steps to change a sentence from passive to active voice:

1. Identify the main verb of the sentence.
2. Identify the real subject by asking, *who performed the action of the verb?*
3. Place the real subject at the beginning of the sentence.
4. Follow the real subject with the verb, making adjustments for agreement.
5. Complete the sentence with the rest of the information.

Let's use the above "formula" to translate another sentence from passive to active voice:

The merger was rejected by their new director.

1.	What's the main verb?	rejected
2.	Who was *doing the rejecting?*	their new director
3.	Begin the sentence with the real subject:	Their new director …
4.	Follow the real subject with the verb:	Their new director rejected …
5.	Complete the sentence:	Their new director rejected the merger.

In the **passive voice**, the structure is: *What was done by whom and why.*

In the **active voice**, the structure is: *Who did what and why.*

Activity 4.5

Active Voice

Instructions: Revise the following sentences to **active voice**.

- Identify the verb.
- Identify the real subject.
- Real Subject – Verb – Object: Who *did / does / will do* what.

For example:

Passive Voice: The inventory <u>was completed</u> by Bob.

Who completed the inventory? Bob (real subject)

Active Voice: Bob completed the inventory.

1. The appointment must have been canceled by one of the clients.

2. The check should have been deposited yesterday to avoid an overdraft.

3. Your papers should have been sent last week.

4. These papers should be filled out and returned by July 15.

5. Your request may be approved by the supervisor this week.

6. A copy of the report will be sent to you tomorrow.

7. The check was endorsed by Juan.

8. You and your staff were being praised by everyone for such a great job.

9. Your home telephone number was given to me by your secretary.

10. You have been given an incomplete report by the human services department.

11. There have been many complaints by service recipients about that policy.

12. A new policy for travel reimbursement was implemented by our director.

13. Your assistance will be appreciated by our entire task group.

14. The program was cancelled due to lack of interest.

Note: See page 217 for the key to this activity.

Nominalization

A **nominalization** is a noun that was originally a verb. For example, the verb *appreciate* becomes *appreciation* in its nominalized form. Using a nominal often makes writing more complicated.

> **Nominalized:** I want to express my **appreciation** for your help.
>
> **Active:** I **appreciate** your help.

As in the example above, the nominal may displace an action verb, replacing it with a "weak verb" (such as make, give, have). Thus, using nominalizations encourages complicated, passive writing. Sometimes writers prefer to use nominalizations because they think using longer, more challenging words sounds smarter. However, as a writer, *your goal* is to make complex messages as *simple* as you can.

Though there is no exact formula, most nominalizations are formed by adding *tion* or *ment* to the base of the verb. Here are a few examples:

Verb	Nominalization	Verb	Nominalization
transport	transportation	encourage	encouragement
develop	development	accomplish	accomplishment
dedicate	dedication	validate	validation
separate	separation	evaluate	evaluation

Some nominalizations are formed in unique ways:

Verb	Nominalization
analyze	analysis
criticize	criticism
believe	belief

At times, nominalizations are necessary; however, use them only when they improve the efficiency and quality of your writing. When nominalizations do not improve the writing, the reader has a more difficult time decoding the message. Here is an example using "negotiate" and "negotiation":

Nominal: The **negotiation** between the attorney and client lasted for hours.

Active: The attorney and client **negotiated** for hours.

Activity 4.6

Nominalization

Instructions: Rewrite the sentences by changing the nominal into the active form of the verb. Some sentences may also need to be changed from passive to active.

Nominalized:	The *distribution* of the list was made by Margaret.
Revised:	Margaret *distributed* the list.

1. The director completed the implementation of the dress policy last August.

2. A suggestion was made by our human resource department that meetings be rescheduled.

3. Their broker gave us information about our new insurance policy.

4. Will there be a discussion of the new resource at our next task group meeting?

5. Our director made an announcement about the grant being funded in the October meeting.

6. The invitation to the conference was given to our department by Alyssa.

7. Martha's decision about the new computers will be made by Friday.

8. The investigation of the missing computers is being done by Michael.

9. If the assistant would make an adjustment in the schedule, we would have better hours.

10. My supervisor gave a recommendation that I arrive to work on time.

Note: See page 218 for the key to this activity.

Posttest

Instructions: Identify and correct the errors in the following sentences.

1. My supervisor had spoke about this policy in a previous meeting.

2. Jessica says that you were unable to assist us with this project.

3. The report include a discussion of our current projects.

4. I would accept the position if I was you.

5. We cannot make additional purchases because our budget is froze until next year.

6. Len address the problem last month.

7. If Margo would of went to the conference, she would have the update.

8. Austin had gave the report to the committee.

9. You should've wrote about the incident shortly after it happened.

10. Each member of the committee attend all meetings.

Note: See page 218 for the key to this posttest.

Irregular Verb Chart

Base Form	Past Tense	Past Participle
arise	arose	arisen
become	became	become
break	broke	broken
bring	brought	brought
buy	bought	bought
choose	chose	chosen
dive	dived, dove	dived
do	did	done
draw	drew	drawn
drink	drank	drunk
drive	drove	driven
eat	ate	eaten
fall	fell	fallen
find	found	found
fly	flew	flown
forget	forgot	forgotten
freeze	froze	frozen
get	got	got, gotten
give	gave	given
go	went	gone
grow	grew	grown
know	knew	known
lend	lent	lent
lose	lost	lost
prove	proved	proved, proven
ride	rode	ridden
say	said	said
see	saw	seen
set	set	set
sink	sank	sunk
sit	sat	sat
show	showed	showed, shown
speak	spoke	spoken
stand	stood	stood
swim	swam	swum
take	took	taken
throw	threw	thrown
wear	wore	worn
write	wrote	written

Notes

5

Use Pronouns Correctly

Most people aren't aware of the mistakes that they make with pronouns, so keep an open mind as you go through this chapter. You see, you may be feeling quite confident as you *err* in your use of common pronouns, for example:

- Is it "between you and *I*" or "between you and *me*"?

- Should you give the report to "John and *myself*" or to "John and *me*" or to "John and *I*?

Unsure speakers pick up incorrect pronoun use unconsciously because the error "sounds right." Since pronouns are a core element of everything that you write, you will struggle with pronouns until you find your comfort zone with them. Finding your comfort zone with pronouns entails using them consciously and consistently.

- First, learn to use pronoun case correctly.

- Second, focus on pronoun-antecedent agreement, making sure that your pronouns agree in number and gender with their antecedents.

- Finally, learn to write *consistently*, staying in the same voice or viewpoint.

The Plan

1. Take the **pretest** on page 72.
2. Complete **Workshop 5 Inventory**, page 72.
3. Review **Part 1: Pronoun Case**; complete Activity 5.1, Pronoun Case, page 76.
4. Review **Part 2: Point of View** and complete all activities (Activities 5.2 through 5.5), pages 77 – 82.
5. Take the **posttest** on page 83; compare pretest and posttest results.
6. To further refine your skills, complete all exercises in Chapter 13, "Pronouns" in *The Writer's Handbook: A Guide for Social Workers* (2014).

Pretest

Instructions: Correct the following sentences for pronoun usage.

1. The social worker said that I could contact Bob or yourself for the information.

2. Louise and him selected the location for the meeting.

3. You should let the issue remain between he and your manager.

4. Send the report to Sylvio and I before you send it to the court.

5. A manager must inform their employees of benefit changes.

6. If her and her supervisor agree, let's go along with the plan.

7. The counselor sent the report to Bob and I, even though we didn't request it.

8. I like taking classes because it improves your skills.

9. If you have more time than me, you should attend the seminar.

10. A project manager should inform others in their group about changes.

Workshop 5 Inventory

1. The pronoun *I* can be used as an object at the end of a sentence.   T/F

2. Pronouns are categorized by cases, note tenses.   T/F

3. For a pair (such as "Bob and I"), to check if using *I* is correct, substitute *we*.   T/F

4. Reflexive pronouns can be used as objects or subjects.   T/F

5. Pronouns sometimes need to agree with their antecedents.   T/F

6. After the conjunction *than,* use a subjective pronoun when the verb is implied.   T/F

7. The possessive pronoun *mine* is never made plural by adding an *s*.   T/F

8. The pronoun *her's* shows possession.   T/F

9. Only use the reflexive pronoun *myself* if it refers back to *I*.   T/F

10. A common mistake with pronouns is using *I* when *me* is correct.   T/F

Note: See page 219 for the key to the pretest and inventory above.

PART 1: PRONOUN CASE

The following chart categorizes personal pronouns based on how they function in a sentence. For example, *subjective pronouns* function as subjects of verbs; *objective pronouns* function as objects of verbs, prepositions, infinitives, and so on.

	Subjective	Objective	Possessive	Reflexive
Singular				
1st Person	I	me	my, mine	myself
2nd Person	you	you	your, yours	yourself
3rd Person	he	him	his	himself
	she	her	hers	herself
	it	it	its	itself
Plural				
1st Person	we	us	our, ours	ourselves
2nd Person	you	you	your, yours	yourselves
3rd Person	they	them	their, theirs	themselves
	who	whom	whose	
	one	one	one's	oneself

Here's how the various cases function in a sentence:

- **Subjective** case pronouns function as **subjects** of verbs, and thus a subjective case pronoun is used as the subject of a sentence.

- **Objective** case pronouns function as **objects,** usually of verbs or prepositions.

- **Possessive** case pronouns **show possession** of nouns or other pronouns.

- **Reflexive** case pronouns reflect back to *subjective case pronouns* and are also known as *intensive case pronouns.*

When using pronouns, people have a tendency to *hypercorrect*, using a formal-sounding pronoun when a less formal-sounding pronoun would be correct. Examples of hypercorrections would include using *I* as an object instead of *me* or perhaps using *myself* when either *I* or *me* would have been correct.

Here are common mistakes that writers and speakers make with *pronoun case*:

Incorrect:	*Her* and her supervisor agree on the issue.
Corrected:	*She* and her supervisor agree on the issue.
Corrected:	*They* agree on the issue.
Incorrect:	The issue is between you and *I*.
Corrected:	The issue is between you and *me*.
Corrected:	The issue is between *us*.

If the pronoun is part of a pair, use the following substitutions:

1. Use *I* if you could substitute *we*, for example: *Sam and I = We*

2. Use *me* if you could substitute *us*, for example: *Sam and me = us.*

3. Use *he* or *she* if you could substitute *they*, for example: *He and Sam = They*

4. Use *him* or *her* if you could substitute *them*, for example: *Sam and him = them*

Another way would be to simplify your sentence by taking out the other person and then testing for sound. Using examples from above, here is how you would test your pronoun based on sound:

Incorrect:	Sam and *me* went to the meeting.
Simplify:	~~Sam and~~ *me* went to the meeting.
Correct:	Sam and *I* went to the meeting.
Incorrect:	Sally asked Sam and *I* for help.
Simplify:	Sally asked ~~Sam and~~ *I* for help.
Correct:	Sally asked Sam and *me* for help.

Pronouns Following *Than*

Most of the time, speakers incorrectly follow the word *than* with an objective case pronoun; the word *than* is a conjunction and may need to be followed by a subject and a verb. Here are examples:

Incorrect:	Mark shoots hoops better than *me.*
Corrected:	Mark shoots hoops better than *I (do).*
Incorrect:	Our department has more work than *them.*
Corrected:	Our department has more work than *they (do).*

If you prefer to be correct without sounding too formal, state the verb at the end of a sentence.

Incorrect:	Mitchell has more time than *me.*
Corrected:	Mitchell has more time than *I have.*

Clarifying Substitutions

- Use *I* if **we** can be substituted for the pair:

  Bob and I are going to the meeting: We are going to the meeting.

  Not: Bob and me are going . . .

- Use **me** if **us** can be substituted for the pair:

  Pat asked Bob and me to go to the meeting: Pat asked us to go.

  Not: Pat asked Bob and I to go to the meeting.

- Use **him** or **her** If **them** can be substituted:

  Pat also asked him and Michelle to go: Pat also asked them to go.

  Not: Pat asked he and Michelle to go.

- Use **he** or **she** If **they** can be substituted:

  He and Michelle went to the meeting: They went to the meeting.

  Not: Him and Michelle went to the meeting.

Activity 5.1

Pronoun Case

Instructions: Circle the correct answer in the sentences below.

1. John and (I, me) completed the project yesterday.

2. Barbara was more competent than (he, him). (*Implied verb?*)

3. Why were the materials delivered to (she, her) and Bob?

4. Dr. Jones said that (us, we) managers should do the work.

5. Between you and (I, me), we have enough expertise.

6. The supervisor required Bob and (I, me, myself) to attend the seminar.

7. You can ask George or (I, myself, me) for the updated report.

8. They are more competent to do the job than (we, us).

9. The attorney asked that the case be divided among you, Alice, and (myself, me).

10. She asked who would do the report, my secretary or (me, myself, I).

11. Margaret is busier than (I, me). (*Implied verb?*)

12. Bill likes Sue better than (I, me). (*Implied verb?*)

13. The professor told my associate and (I, me, myself) to complete our report.

14. The information was sent to (she and I, her and me, her and I).

15. George and (me, I) watched the podcast before (he, him) and (I, me) left.

16. Upon recommendation, he gave the project to Jim and (I, me, myself).

17. Bob has more time than (me, I).

18. The project will be split between John and (I, me, myself).

19. She asked Phyllis and (me, myself) to attend the board meeting.

20. The problem should remain between Bob and (you, yourself).

21. Did Allison and (I, me) cause you a problem?

22. I am going to make (me, myself) an excellent dinner.

23. When he asked, I responded, "It is (I, me)."

Note: See page 220 for the key to this activity.

PART 2: POINT OF VIEW

Point of view refers to the pronoun viewpoint from which a document is written, which can be from *first, second,* or *third person, singular* or *plural.*

For example, when you write from *first person singular*, you write from the *I* viewpoint, an effective viewpoint for writing in a journal. When you write from the second person viewpoint, you write from the *you* viewpoint, speaking directly to the reader, an effective viewpoint for connecting with the reader as in e-mail messages.

Point of View and Voice

Pronoun viewpoint helps define a writer's voice. *Voice* is an element of writing that engages the reader. Voice is an element of all types of writing, not just creative or personal writing, but professional and academic writing as well. In fact, you will find that your voice changes according to the type of writing that you are doing.

- When you write from your *personal voice*, you are expressing your feelings and opinions. Use your personal voice when you write journals and reflections, speaking freely and using the personal pronoun "I," which is the *I* **viewpoint**.

- When you write from your *professional voice*, you are connecting with your readers through simple, clear, concise writing. Use your professional voice when you write e-mail messages, business letters, and memos: focus on using the *you* **point of view** and *limiting your use of the personal pronoun* **I**, *when possible*. (For more detail, see Workshop 7, "Control Your Tone.")

- When you write from your *academic voice*, you are writing in the most formal way, taking ideas and concepts apart, analyzing data, decisions, positions, and actions as well as asking questions in a dispassionate, non-adversarial way. For academic writing, focus on using the **third person point of view,** and avoid, for the most part, the use of the personal pronoun *I*.

Using pronouns correctly enables you to adapt your voice for your audience. As you work through this section, reflect on how pronouns contribute to the tone of writing.

> As you see, pronoun usage is a critical element of voice. Another element, especially for professional and academic writing, is *formatting: formatting speaks to readers at a glance.* For example, format e-mail messages with a greeting and a closing so that you connect effectively with your reader; also cite and format in APA style correctly. By following formatting guidelines, you show respect to your readers.

Pronoun and Antecedent Agreement

Pronouns can be used in place of nouns and other pronouns, and the words that pronouns refer to are known as *antecedents*.

- Pronouns must agree in number and gender with their antecedents.
- Many antecedents are not gender specific, such as *person, doctor, engineer, lawyer, teacher*, and so on, which creates a problem.

In the following example, *managers* is the antecedent of *they* and *their*.

> All *managers* said that *they* would submit *their* quarterly reports by Friday.

Here is another example with *person* and *people* used as *antecedents*:

Incorrect: A *person* must do what *they* are asked.

Corrected: A *person* must do what *he or she* is asked.

   People must do what *they* are asked.

When writers use singular antecedents that are gender neutral, writers must use combinations of pronouns, such as *he/she* or *him/her*.

Correct: When a *lawyer* performs *his* or *her* duties, *he* or *she* must remain attentive to *his* or *her* clients.

When using singular antecedents, writers are prone to errors, for example:

Incorrect: When *a lawyer* performs *their* duties, *they* must remain attentive to *their* clients.

To avoid the awkwardness of using singular pronouns (such as *he or she* or *his or her*) and avoid the type of error shown above, use plural antecedents.

Correct: When *lawyers* perform *their* duties *they* must remain attentive to *their* clients.

Here is another example:

Incorrect: Every *team member* should bring *their* own *laptop*.

Corrected: Every *team member* should bring *his* or *her* own *laptop.*

All *team members* should bring *their* own *laptops.*

(*You*) bring *your* own laptop.

Notice in the above example that *laptops* becomes plural along with *team members.* Agreement applies to all related elements. At times, when two or more antecedents appear in a sentence, pronoun reference can be unclear. For example, in the following, to which person does the pronoun *she* refer?

> *Sue* and *Martha* completed their report by Tuesday so that *she* could present the findings in a conference on Thursday.

When meaning is unclear, restate the antecedent rather than using a pronoun:

> *Sue* and *Martha* completed their report by Tuesday so that *Martha* could present the findings in a conference on Thursday.

Activity 5.2
Pronoun and Antecedent Agreement

Instructions: Correct the following sentences for pronoun-antecedent agreement.

Incorrect: Ask a friend for their help only when you really need it.

Corrected: Ask *friends* for their help only when you really need it.

1. When an employee calls in sick, they should give a reason.
2. When a social worker does not relate well to their clients, they need more training.
3. A social worker is going beyond their job description when they assist a client's guests.
4. A case manager's job is challenging because they work under difficult conditions.
5. When a customer does not have a receipt, they may not be able to return an item.
6. Charley said that John should be on his team because he would be available during his training.
7. When a person writes reports, they need to stay focused.
8. A case manager needs to stay in touch with their clients.
9. When you ask someone for assistance, they should help or let you know they cannot.
10. A person must do their best when the situation calls for it.

Note: See page 221 for the key to this activity.

Viewpoint and Consistency

Along the lines of pronoun-antecedent agreement, you must also address the issue of consistency of viewpoint. Pronoun viewpoint, or *point of view*, can emanate from first, second, or third person, singular or plural.

	Singular	**Plural**
First Person	I	We
Second Person	You	You
Third Person	A person	People

Here are examples of the various viewpoints:

When *I* write, *I* must pay attention to *my* audience.

When *you* write, *you* must pay attention to *your* audience.

When a *person* writes, *he* or *she* must pay attention to *his* or *her* audience.

When *we* write, *we* must pay attention to *our* audience.

When *people* write, *they* must pay attention to *their* audience.

When *one* writes, *one* must pay attention to *one's* audience.

Though the *one* viewpoint is not common in the United States, other English-speaking countries commonly use the *one* viewpoint. An error many writers make, however, is to use the pronoun *one* when they are unsure, for example:

Incorrect: *I* think *one* should write daily because *you* improve *your* skills.

Incorrect: If *one* arrives on time, *they* will receive prompt service.

As you compose, write freely. However, when you edit, screen your work for correct usage, consistency, and agreement: Do not shift point of view within sentences or even entire paragraphs. Here is how the above sentences could be written:

Corrected: *I* should write daily because *I* will improve *my* skills.

Corrected: If *you* arrive on time, *you* will receive prompt service.

The key point here is that when you are writing longer pieces, such as paragraphs and papers, *stay within the same point of view throughout.*

When writing instructions, use the *you* viewpoint and stay in the active voice:

> (You) Fill out the application immediately so that you are eligible for benefits.
>
> (You) Answer all questions completely.
>
> (You) Send your application by October 15.

Point of view helps you adapt your topic for your audience. Once you select a point of view, the key is using it consistently. Edit individual sentences and individual paragraphs for consistency as well as entire documents.

Activity 5.3

Consistent Point of View

Instructions: Correct the following sentences for pronoun-antecedent agreement. You can correct each sentence in various viewpoints—the key is consistency, **for example**:

Incorrect: A person who does their best will achieve the best possible outcome.

Corrected: A person who does *his or her* best will achieve the best possible outcome.

People who do *their* best will achieve the best possible outcome.

If *you* do *your* best, *you* will achieve the best possible outcome.

1. A supervisor should consider various ways they will deal with personnel problems.

2. One sometimes thinks another situation is better until you experience it.

3. We generally follow the rules unless you are told otherwise.

4. If a person is conscientious, they will do well in their jobs.

5. One does not always follow instructions, but we should.

6. A person should strive to get a great education so you can have a satisfying career.

7. Trying one's hardest to get in good shape can ruin your health if you're not careful.

8. Everyone must make their own reservations.

9. Sue went to the meeting with Mary to ensure that she gave a complete report.

10. Neither of the managers gave their department the memo.

Note: See page 222 for the key to this activity.

Activity 5.4

Pronoun Consistency

Instructions: Edit the following paragraph, screening for pronoun consistency.

For example: *I*

I enjoy going to meetings because ~~you~~ find out about current projects.

I enjoy working on team projects because you learn so much from your teammates. A team member needs to be supportive because they never know when they will need assistance from his or her colleagues. When you are on a team, every member needs to carry their weight. That is, if one would not do his or her share of the work can, they can be a burden to the team and jeopardize their project.

If a team member stays motivated, you are more valuable to the team. I always strive to do my best because you never know when you will need to count on your team members.

Activity 5.5

Pronoun and Antecedent Agreement

Instructions: In the following paragraph, correct the pronouns and their antecedents and develop a *consistent point of view.*

For example: *New applicants need*

~~A new applicant needs~~ to fill out their tax forms.

A new applicant must understand that you will experience a period of adjustment at their new program. Unfortunately, many new participants think that one's fellow participants should adjust to you instead of the other way around. When you begin a new program, one should "lay low" for the first few months to learn the way the work environment functions. After one has held a position for three or four months, you can begin making appropriate suggestions and changes.

Note: See pages 222 and 223 for the keys to the above activities.

Posttest

Instructions: Correct the following sentences for pronoun usage.

1. You can contact Bob or myself for assistance with the project.

2. Him and his supervisor selected the topic for the conference.

3. Yours are on the table; her's are in the conference room.

4. You should let the issue remain between he and your co-worker.

5. Send the report to Jeff and I before you pass it on to anyone else.

6. A social worker must inform their clients of the limits to confidentiality.

7. If her and her partner agree, let's go along with the plan.

8. The agency sent the report to Bob and I, even though we didn't request it.

9. You can rely on there instructions in getting the job done effectively.

10. If you have more time than me, you should attend the seminar.

Note: See page 223 for the key to this posttest.

Notes

6

Be Concise

To get rid of the clutter in your writing, you may need to change some ways of thinking, giving up some security blankets. This chapter shows you how to make painful cuts for sake of clarity, applying the following principle:

Less is more.

Simple words and short messages convey information more effectively than complex words and long messages, and using big, four-syllable words is *not* a sign of intelligence.

When you edit, cut redundant words, unnecessary explanations, and outdated expressions so that your key points stand out.

Workshop 6 Inventory

Instructions: Read and answer the questions below.

1. Complicated, four-syllable words make a writer sound smart.   T/F

2. When you request a favor, use the phrase "thank you in advance."   T/F

3. To refer to a previous conversation, use the phrase, "per our conversation."   T/F

4. Even lawyers should avoid legalese.   T/F

5. Certain redundant phrases have been in use for centuries.   T/F

6. When attaching a document, use the phrase "attached please find."   T/F

7. Background thinking helps readers understand the intent of your message.   T/F

8. "Subsequent to" sounds more sophisticated than "after."   T/F

9. Simple language is more effective than complicated language.   T/F

10. When you use complicated language, it makes you sound smart.   T/F

Note: See page 223 for the key to this inventory.

Review the following principles and complete all activities: *the more you practice, the more likely you are to apply principles to your own writing.*

Eliminate Redundant Phrases and Outdated Expressions

Which of the following redundant and outdated expressions do you use?

Completely eliminate the problem.	*Eliminate* the problem.
That was a *terrible tragedy.*	That was a *tragedy.*
His book was *cheaper in cost.*	His book was *cheaper.*
Her suit is *red in color.*	Her suit is *red.*
As *per* your request . . .	As you requested . . .
Attached please find the requested form.	The form you requested *is attached.*
Thank you in advance for your assistance.	*Thank you* for assisting us.

"Per" is a Latin term. The following is an example of how to use it correctly:

The cost of the room *per diem* is $200.

Notice that *per diem* is italicized because it is a foreign term, and all foreign terms should be italicized.

Choose Simple Language

Whether you choose simple words or more complicated ones also affects the tone of your document. When possible, use a simple word instead of a complicated one. Here are a few examples:

We *utilize* the best methods.	We *use* the best methods.
Our manager is *cognizant of* the policy	Our manager *knows* the policy.
We *endeavor* to give effective service.	We *try* to give effective service.
Their decision is *contingent upon his reaction.*	Their decision *depends on how he reacts.*
Prior to their involvement, we made progress.	*Before they became involved*, we made progress.

Activity 6.1

Avoid Redundancy—Eliminate Unnecessary Words

Instructions: *Cover the right side of the page,* and then revise the phrases in the left column, **for example:**

Redundant	**Revised:**
written down	written
as per our discussion	as we discussed

Redundant		**Revised**
completely eliminate	_____	eliminate
added bonus	_____	bonus
collaborate together	_____	collaborate
advanced reservations	_____	reservations
spell out in detail	_____	spell out or detail
therapeutic treatment	_____	treatment
actual experience	_____	experience
unintended mistake	_____	mistake
depreciate in value	_____	depreciate
important essentials	_____	essentials
free gift	_____	free or a gift

Wordy/Outdated		**Revised**
as per your request	_____	as (you) requested
thank you in advance	_____	thank you
in receipt of	_____	received
subsequent to	_____	after
in the near future	_____	soon
attached please find	_____	attached is
due to the fact that	_____	because
to advise you	_____	to let you know
to whom it may concern	_____	[find out the person's name or use a title]

Activity 6.2

Replace Wordy and Outdated Language

Instructions: Match the following words to the wordy and outdated phrases below.

A. possible   D. before   G. always   J. because

B. helped   E. about   H. now   K. soon

C. if   F. while   I. noon or 12 p.m. L. believes

_____ 1. due to the fact that   _____ 7. is of the opinion that

_____ 2. in the event that   _____ 8. 12 noon

_____ 3. in reference to   _____ 9. at the present time

_____ 4. within the realm of possibility   _____ 10. at all times

_____ 5. during the time that   _____ 11. prior to

_____ 6. gave assistance to   _____ 12. at your earliest convenience

Activity 6.3

Remove Redundancy from Paired Expressions and Modifiers

Instructions: In the expressions below, delete the redundancy, **for example:**

Paired Expressions	**Needless Modifiers**
~~full and~~ complete	~~free~~ gift

Paired Expressions	**Modifiers**
true and accurate	false pretense
each and every	true facts
hope and trust	future plans
first and foremost	personal beliefs
various and sundry	consensus of opinion
any and all	sudden crisis
questions and problems	completely finish
over and done with	direct confrontation
confusing and unclear	end result
forever and ever	final outcome
and so on and so forth	initial preparation
	tuna fish

Note: See page 224 for the key to the above activities.

Replace Formal Words with More Common Words

Which of the following formal words do you need to replace with more common ones?

Formal	**Common**
contingent upon	dependent on
implement	start, begin
endeavor	try
deem	think
utilization	use
apprise	inform
termination	end
transpire	happen
initiate	begin
render	make, give
is desirous of	wants
disseminate	send out
strategize	plan
cognizant of	aware of
prior to	before
ascertain	find out
facilitate	help
subsequent to	after

Are there formal words that you feel the need to continue to use?

Avoid Dated Expressions

Which of the following redundant and outdated expressions do you use?

At your earliest convenience	Give a specific date.
Looking forward to hearing from you.	*I look forward to hearing from you.*
Thank you in advance	Simply say *Thank you.*
Thank you again	One *thank you* is sufficient.
Pursuant to	Legalistic terms belong to lawyers.
With regard to	Say *about* or *concerning.*
In receipt of	Instead say *thank you for* . . .
As per our discussion	*As we discussed* . . .
I wish to thank you	Don't wish and thank.

Activity 6.4

Get Rid of Empty, Redundant, and Outdated Language

Instructions: With a partner, simplify the following sentences and remove **empty information**, **redundancy**, and **outdated expressions**.

Weak:	We will ascertain the cause of the problem and correct it immediately.
Revised:	We will find out the cause the problem and correct it immediately.

1. Enclosed please find the papers that were requested by you.

2. Your complete and absolute confidence in our approach is appreciated.

3. As per our discussion, the new policy should be received by you this week.

4. You can completely eliminate one step in the process by using a cover that is green in color.

5. I would like to thank you in advance for your consideration of my application.

6. Per your request, the application for admission to our program has been enclosed.

7. The decision for the utilization of that approach with the children was made by your wife.

8. Subsequent to their involvement, we made little progress.

9. Always endeavor to do your best, especially when you are cognizant of the challenges.

10. A free gift has been sent out to you because of your fast and prompt response to our survey.

11. Per our conversation, we will completely finish the preparations for the June conference by the deadline.

12. Attached please find the report, which I am sending per your request.

Note: See page 225 for the key to this activity.

Edit Out Background Thinking, Feelings, and Opinions

Background thinking consists of telling *how* you arrived at your conclusions. Background thinking is different from explaining an issue or giving evidence to support a point.

Activity 6.5

Editing for Background Thinking

Instructions: Edit the following message by removing background information.

After giving much thought to our discussion about the situation, I realized I might find some answers by doing some informal research. I first called several of our colleagues, but none of them had heard of this type of situation before. Although I was discouraged, I continued to search. That's when I realized that I could go right to the supervisor. I checked with her and found out that she has used a similar type of approach with several families.

Activity 6.6

Editing to Get to the Point

Instructions: Edit the following message by removing background information.

After we spoke, I continued to think about the situation in which we find ourselves. Not that long ago, the economy was strong, and we were able to provide services on a sliding-fee. Now, with the sudden change in the economy, we are faced with uncertainty—many of our clients will be tightening their belts and reducing their spending. The point that I am trying to make is that we need to make changes to make up for our losses. Rather than simply raising our fees, I think it would a good idea consult with other agencies. What do you think?

Note: See page 226 for suggested keys to the above activities.

Do not tell your reader *how* to interpret your message; these added comments may give the reader the impression that you are unsure of your message or that you lack confidence. Thus, remove phrases or sentences that tell your readers *how you think* they will react.

Activity 6.7

Editing to Stay on Point

Instructions: Edit the following message by removing background information.

I'm not sure if you will be interested in the information in this message about this referral, but I am sending it along just in case this could help you with the current project you are working on. I know you are under a lot of pressure to make progress with a project relating to your job. So, just to reassure you, I'm only suggesting that you contact my referral because I know that she has encountered similar situations and can really help you. Her name is Cynthia Baker, and her number is (555) 123-5555.

Note: See page 226 for a suggested key to the above activity.

Notes

7

Control Your Tone

Tone reflects the emotions of writing: tone is not as much about *what* you say as about *how* you say it. Your tone can either build up a relationship or tear it down, and you may not even realize it.

Keep your mind open to the fact that just as there are at least two sides to every story, there are two sides to tone:

> Tone is just as much about the way that a reader *interprets* a message
> as it is about the way that a writer *conveys* a message.

Two principles that affect tone are the *you* viewpoint and *writing in the affirmative*, also referred to as *keeping a positive focus*.

Workshop 7 Inventory

Instructions: Read and answer the questions below.

1. The *you* viewpoint helps you connect more effectively with a client than does the *I* viewpoint.   T/F
2. When you are having a difficult conversation, focus on using the *I* viewpoint.   T/F
3. Most negative statements can be made in the affirmative.   T/F
4. People respond more positively to statements made in the affirmative as compared to the same statements made in the negative.   T/F
5. The best time to shift to the *you* viewpoint is when you edit.   T/F
6. Negative comments are likely to be met with more resistance than the same message stated in the positive.   T/F
7. The *you* viewpoint and affirmative writing have a strong impact on tone.   T/F
8. At times, the *I* viewpoint is necessary.   T/F

Note: See page 226 for the key to this inventory.

The *You* Point of View

As you compose a message, you are writing for yourself because you are in the midst of understanding your purpose and the points you wish to make. You may find that many sentences are formed from the *I* point of view. In other words, you may write sentences such as the following:

> I am writing you to ask if you would be able to attend a meeting on Friday.
>
> I am happy to hear that you are doing well on your new job.
>
> I have a few questions that I would like to pass by for your feedback.

When you write from the *I* point of view, you keep focus on yourself. However, when you focus on your reader rather than yourself, you set a more effective, reader-friendly tone. For example,

> Would *you* be able to attend a meeting on Friday?
>
> Congratulations for doing so well on your new job.
>
> Would *you* answer a few questions for me? Your feedback is valuable.

The *I viewpoint* implies ownership and, at times, is necessary: do not try to revise a sentence to the *you viewpoint* if it results in an awkward sentence. In addition, if you are speaking about a sensitive issue, speak from your own point of view, for example:

You Viewpoint: You are making me feel very uncomfortable.

I Viewpoint: I am feeling uncomfortable with the situation.

Also, do not use the *you* viewpoint if it sounds as if you are pointing blame:

Awkward: You did not send your papers by the deadline.

Revised: I did not receive your papers by the deadline.

Do not focus on point of view as you compose. When you edit, changes sentences to the appropriate viewpoint, whether that be the *I viewpoint* or the *you viewpoint.*

I Viewpoint: I don't know anyone who can do this kind of job better than you.

You Viewpoint: You are the best person for the job.

I Viewpoint: I would like to invite you to our next meeting.

You Viewpoint: You are welcome to attend our next meeting.

Activity 7.1

The *You* Viewpoint

Instructions: Adjust the tone of the following sentences to the ***you viewpoint***.

Weak: I hope that you are doing well.

Revised: How are you doing?

1. I would like to inform you that your input made a difference in our decision.

2. We are asking that the completed application be returned within five days.

3. I have received your proposal within the deadline.

4. I would like to invite you to our next team meeting.

5. I am interested in learning more about your new project.

6. It seems to me that you are well qualified for the new position.

7. I respect your opinions and hope to continue to receive them.

8. I am hoping to include you on the list of advisors for the new project.

9. I would appreciate if you would do me a favor.

10. I wanted to tell you that I am happy with your new report.

Activity 7.2

The *You* Viewpoint

Instructions: At times, the you viewpoint can sound awkward. Revise the following sentences to a viewpoint that sounds more objective.

Awkward: Your comment made the problem worse.

Revised: When the comment was made, the situation became more challenging.

1. If you wanted your paper to be considered, you should have sent it by the deadline.

2. To avoid an overdraft, you should have deposited funds to your account yesterday.

3. When you made that remark, you were offensive.

Note: See page 227 for the key to the above activities.

A Positive Focus

Everyone appreciates positive words; even subtle comments add energy. In writing, you help set a positive tone by describing situations in affirmative language.

In other words, rather than saying what will go wrong if procedures are *not* followed, *say what will go right if the procedures are followed.*

Here are some examples:

Negative: If you do not return this within 10 days, your benefits will be delayed.

Positive: If you return this within 10 days, your benefits will start immediately.

Negative: If you do not respond by Friday, I will not be able to use your input.

Positive: Only if you respond by Friday will I be able to use your input.

Negative: By not going to the meeting, you will miss important information.

Positive: By going to the meeting, you will learn valuable information.

Thus, focus on what will to right if things are done according to plan rather than what will go wrong if things are not done accordingly. It sounds less threatening to the listener or the reader.

What are some examples of times when you had to say "no"? For example, "No, I cannot go to the meeting," and so on.

(When you are finished with Activity 7.3, revisit your examples to see if you would phrase them differently.)

Writing in the Affirmative

Writing in the affirmative takes fewer words and keeps information more simple and sometimes more positive, important qualities in business. Here are some examples:

William **did not remember** the agenda.	William **forgot** the agenda.
It is obvious that he **will not be on time**.	He **will be late**.
The messages are **not the same**.	The messages are **different.**
She **does not have** the resources.	She **lacks** the resources.
	Or: She **needs additional** resources.

Activity 7.3

A Positive Focus

Instructions: The goal of this exercise is to give a response without saying "no": try to come up with a response that sounds positive or is written in the affirmative.

Weak:	If you don't answer my questions, I can't help you.
Revised:	If you answer my questions, I will be able to help you.

Weak:	I didn't meet your deadline.
Revised:	I'm still working on the project and will have it to you today by noon. I appreciate your patience.

1. Do not arrive before noon.

2. I don't have time right now.

3. Here's what happened—J. R. called in sick, and I was shorthanded with lots of other priorities.

4. Your credentials do not meet our requirements for the position funded by the grant proposal.

5. We are behind schedule, and we cannot complete your project by the requested date, July 15.

6. I have not received a response from you for two days, and I need the information now! I know that you carry around an iPhone—why haven't you answered me???

7. When you are late, the meetings don't run smoothly.

8. That's not my job—you'll have to speak to someone else.

9. No, I can't help you with this—it's our policy that we cannot divulge that type of information over the phone.

10. Do not write in the negative.

Note: See page 228 for the key to this activity.

A *Thinker* or *Feeler* Approach

Another element of tone involves how much feeling—or lack of feeling (often called "abruptness")—writers put into their messages.

One of the major categories on the Meyers-Briggs is the *thinking-feeling* category. Scoring high on either *thinking* or *feeling* will influence how a writer approaches a task. *Thinkers* tend to base their decisions on hard data without considering emotional factors. *Feelers,* on the other hand, consider emotional factors a priority. Neither approach is right or wrong; however, a balanced approach is more effective.

Thinker Approach: Getting right to the point and making little or no effort to connect with the reader as one human to another.

Feeler Approach: Placing more emphasis on connecting to the reader than to the information being conveyed.

While *thinkers* take a straightforward approach, *feelers* have the urge to be social and friendly. *Thinkers* resist using fluff and niceties, but *feelers* search out ways to express things other than their direct message. Of course, everyone exhibits characteristics of each type; personality type is a matter of degree. Whether you're a *thinker* or a *feeler, the key is to find a balance between the two.*

Thinker message: We need additional forms. Please send them now.

Feeler message: Hi, Jorge. Hope your day is going well. I just wanted you to know that we need more forms. If it isn't too much trouble, I'd appreciate if you could help me with this. Thank you so much.

Balanced message: Hi Jorge,

Could you please send me some additional forms. If you could send them today, that would be great. Thank you.

Notes

8

Use Words Effectively

English has many common words that confuse writers, such as *its* and *it's* or *affect* and *effect*. These kinds of words are called *similar words* or *homophones*—they sound alike but are spelled differently and have different meanings.

Like any skill, the only way to build your vocabulary is through practice and repetition. Use new words in context, and you are more likely to remember them. To get started, take the pretest below to identify the words that you need to work on.

Pretest: Similar Words

Instructions: In the sentences below, cross out any words that are used incorrectly, and write in the correct word above it or to the right of the sentence.

1. Will that decision effect you in a positive way?
2. The principle on my loan is due on the 1st of the month.
3. My advise is for you to get a job before you buy that new car.
4. Please ensure my supervisor that I will return in one-half hour.
5. Its been a challenging day, but things are getting better.
6. Their are a few issues that we need to discuss.
7. Pat lives further from work than I do.
8. You can have a meeting everyday, if you prefer.
9. I enjoy working with children more then I enjoy working with teenagers.
10. Megan assured that the project would be successful
11. It's alright for you to contact the social worker directly.
12. I didn't mean to infer that you were late on purpose.
13. Try and be on time for the next meeting.
14. We wondered weather you where coming.
15. I like your ideal of going to the conference.

Note: See page 229 for the key to this pretest.

Tricky Combos

Are you ready for some surprises? In all likelihood, you have been using some words incorrectly without any clue they were wrong. Work through the lists below, referring to Chapter 19, "Word Usage" in *The Writer's Handbook* as needed.

Instructions: For the words that give you challenges, write two or three sentences to gain practice using them correctly.

alright/all right:

- The word "alright" is not considered a Standard English spelling.
- Use *all right*. Think of *all right* as being the opposite of *all wrong*.

Example: Are you feeling *all right* about the change?

idea/ideal:

- An *idea* is a thought; an opinion, conviction, principle.
- *Ideal* refers to a standard of perfection.

Examples: I had a good *idea* the other day. What is your *idea*?

The *ideal* solution does not exist.

Titus lives by his *ideals*, which is why he always does his best.

loan/lend: Most people confuse these words and don't even realize it, even people in high level banking positions! Here is what you need to know:

- *Loan* is a *noun*, not an action.
- *Lend* is a *verb*; its past tense form is "lent."

Example: The bank will *lend* you the funds you need by giving you a *loan*.

Though you cannot "loan" someone your book, you can *lend* it. Practice these words a few times, and their meanings will make more sense each time you use them correctly.

may be/maybe:

- *May be* is a verb form that suggests possibility.
- *Maybe* is an adverb that means "perhaps."

Example: I *may be* presenting at this week's meeting; *maybe* you can assist.

principal/principle: At one point, you may have learned that the *principal* of your school was your "pal." That's true; however, *principal* has a broader meaning:

- *Principal* is a noun meaning "the person with the highest authority," but it is also an adjective meaning "primary, predominant, or main." Are you surprised to learn that in paying back a loan, you must pay your "*principal* and interest."
- *Principle* means "theory or rule of conduct."

Examples: What is the *principal* on your loan?

We all try to live by our *principles*.

I would rather pay off my *principal* than continue to pay interest!

weather/whether:

- *Weather* is usually a noun, referring to the temperature and atmospheric conditions.
- *Weather* can be a verb that figuratively means "to live through."
- *Whether* is a conjunction that introduces possibilities or alternatives

Examples: The *weather* is beautiful today: it's sunny and cool.

Would you let me know *whether* or not you can attend the meeting?

Though we had challenges, we weathered

were/where:

- *Were* is a verb (a past time form of the verb *to be*)
- *Where* is an adverb

Examples: *Were* you in the meeting? If not, *where were* you?

Where were you when the lights went out?

Tricky Verbs

If you have challenges with contractions, stop using them and spell out words completely. However, when you use contractions, use an apostrophe: writers lose credibility when they make those kinds of misspellings; for example, for *do not*, the contraction is "don't" not "dont"!

affect/effect: Though each of these words can be a noun and a verb, here's their primary use:

- *Affect* is a verb meaning "to influence."
- *Effect* is a noun meaning "result."

As a noun, *affect* refers to emotions and is used primarily within the field of mental health; as a verb, *effect* means "to cause to happen" or "to bring about."

Examples: My sister was diagnosed with an *affective* (emotional) disorder.

The new policy will *effect* (bring about) change within our agency.

assure/ensure/insure: These three verbs are somewhat similar in sound and meaning, but they have distinct uses:

- *Assure* means "to give *someone* confidence."
- *Ensure* means "to make certain" that *something* will happen.
- *Insure* means "to protect against loss."

Examples: When you use *assure*, make sure that a "person" is the object:

I *assure* you that we will do everything we can.

When you use *ensure*, make sure that a "thing" is the object:

I *ensure* that the grant proposal will arrive on time.

When you use *insure*, make sure that it refers to "insurance."

You can *insure* against losses with our company.

don't/doesn't:

- *Don't* and *doesn't* are both contractions of *do not*.

- At times speakers use *don't* for third person singular when they should be using *doesn't* for correct Edited American English usage.

- APA does not accept contractions; however, you can use contractions in less formal writing, such as e-mail messages.

- Spelling a contraction without an apostrophe (such as "dont" for "don't") is a serious spelling error that can cause a writer to lose credibility.

Examples: Alice *does not* like math, and she *doesn't* like history either.

has/have: Developing writers sometimes use *have* for third person singular when they should be using *has*.

- *Has* and *have* are both present tense forms of *to have*.

- Use *has* for third person singular (he *has*, she *has*, and it *has*) and *have* for all other persons: I *have*, you *have*, we *have* and they *have*.

Example: Rob *has* an exam on Friday.
We *have* an exam every Friday.

Infer/imply: These two verbs are opposite in meaning.

- *Infer* means to *deduce, conclude,* or *assume.*

- *Imply* means to *express* or *state indirectly.*

Example: The client *implied* that she needed money.
I *inferred* that she was telling the truth.

Tricky Pronouns

For the words that give you challenges, write a few sentences using them correctly. You can even start by writing a sentence using the word incorrectly and then revise it using the correct spelling. Here's an example using "it's":

Incorrect: Its time to start the meeting.

Corrected: It's time to start the meeting. OR: It is time to start the meeting.

its/it's:

- *Its* is a possessive pronoun
- *It's* is a contraction of *it is* or *it has*.

Examples: *It's* a beautiful day for a walk.

The project lost *its* appeal after the chairperson resigned.

their/there/they're:

- *Their* is the possessive form of *they* and will always be followed by a noun.
- *There* is an adverb meaning "in or at *that* place" or a pronoun which functions as an anticipating subject.
- *They're* is the contracted form of *they are*.

Examples: *Their* car would not start.

Put the file over *there*.

There are many issues to discuss.

They're running late today.

who's/whose:

- The contraction *who's* stands for *who is* or *who has*.
- *Whose* is the possessive pronoun of *who*.

Examples: *Who's* (who is) submitting the proposal?

Whose turn is it to chair the meeting?

you're/your:

- *You're* is a contraction for *you are*.
- *Your* is a possessive pronoun for *you*.

Examples: *You're* the best person for the job.

Your opinion matters.

Tricky Prepositions

A preposition often precedes a noun or pronoun and indicates a relation of one word to another.

among/between:

- *Among* is a preposition meaning *together with* or *along with* and is used when three or more people or objects are involved.

- *Between* is a preposition that means basically the same thing as *among*, but *between* is used when two people or objects are discussed.

Examples: *Between* you and me, we should be able to get the job done.

Among all of the applicants, Jose did the best.

through/threw/thorough/thru:

- *Through* is a preposition meaning *by means of, from beginning to end*, or *because of*.

- *Threw* is a verb and the past participle of *throw*.

- *Thorough* is an adjective meaning *carried through to completion*.

- *Note: Thru* is a "word" that does not exist in Standard English—use it only as a part of the term "drive-thru."

Examples: When you go *through* the door, be careful.

Billy *threw* the ball to Alice.

Do a *thorough* job on the report.

If you need a quick meal, go *through* a drive-*thru*.

to/too: The preposition *to* is often used when the adverb *too* is appropriate.

- Use the adverb *too* the adverb when you are describing something that relates to quantity. Also use *too* when you could substitute the word *also*.

Examples: I have *too* much work to do and *too* little time in which to do it.

Would you like to go to the meeting *too*?

If he has *too* many concerns, we should cancel the project.

Do you feel that way *too*?

Going to the conference after working all day was *too* much.

More Similar Words

Which of the following give you challenges?

advice/advise:

- *Advice* is a noun and means *recommendation*.
- *Advise* is a verb and it means *to give advice or to make a recommendation*.

Examples: I *advise* you to listen to your supervisor's *advice*.

appraise/apprise:

- *Appraise* is a verb meaning *to assess* or *evaluate*.
- *Apprise* is a verb meaning *to inform*.

Example: After you *appraise* the situation, *apprise* us of your results.

customer/costumer

- A *customer* is a *client, patron*.
- A *costumer* is a person who makes costumes for theater and films.

Example: The word *customer* is sometimes spelled incorrectly as *costumer*, possibly due to subtleties in pronunciation.

definite/defiant:

- *Definite* is adjective meaning *sure, exact*, or *significant*.
- *Defiant* is an adjective that means *disobedient, insolent*, or *insubordinate*.

Examples: Marcel has *definite* ideas about how to handle the situation.
His employee was *defiant* about getting the job done right.

everyday/every day:

- Use *everyday* as a modifier meaning "ordinary" or "daily."
- Use *every day* if you can insert the word "single" between *every* and *day*.

Examples: Answering messages is an *everyday* activity on the job.
You will hear from me *every (single) day* this week.

farther/further:

- *Farther* refers to actual distance that can be measured.
- *Further* indicates progress that is intangible and not measurable, such as "to a greater or lesser degree or extent."

Examples: I live *farther* from work than you do by at least 5 miles.

We are *further* along on the project than we realize.

sight/site/cite:

- *Sight* is a noun referring to vision or mental perception.
- *Site* is also a noun that refers to a location, as in website.
- *Cite* is a verb meaning *to quote* or *to name.*

Examples: Sue's favorite saying is, "Out of *sight*, out of mind."

Our agency does all of its training on *site.*

Cite your references correctly according to APA style.

supposed to/used to: Because speakers do not always pronounce words clearly, the past time ending is sometimes erroneously left off when these words are written.

- *Supposed to* and *used to* are regular verbs in past tense and require the –ed ending.

Examples: I am *supposed to* take Friday as a vacation day.

Tanya *used to* work in my agency.

than/then:

- *Than* is a conjunction used in comparisons.
- *Then* is an adverb referring to time, as in "after that." To help remember, use *then* when it has to do with a "*when.*"

Examples   I would rather go to the meeting *than* work on the report.

I will go to the meeting and *then* work on the report.

try to/"try and": The verb *try* is followed by an infinitive, such *to be, to see, to go,* and so on. In other words, do *not* use the construction "try and."

Examples: *Try to be* on time. Also, *try to* relax when you give your presentation.

Activity 8.1: Similar Words

Instructions: In the sentences below, circle the correct word.

1. They have (to, too) many new projects and (to, too) little time.
2. You will be (appraised, apprised) of the situation before noon today.
3. Jackson (assured, ensured) me that you got the job.
4. The file documented that she felt (alright, all right) about the change.
5. (Your, you're) the right person to turn the situation around.
6. (Among, Between) the three of us, we have all the resources we need.
7. Try (and, to) see Leonard before you leave today.
8. Kevin said that he would (loan, lend) me his notes.
9. His remark was a real (complement, compliment).
10. The father lives (farther, further) from work (than, then) the mother does.
11. If you (could of, could have) spoken to Della, you'd understand.
12. Vera (past, passed) that cold on to her daughters (to, too).
13. How will that (affect, effect) you?
14. When you know the (affect, effect), let me know.
15. Carol (loaned, lent) me everything I needed for the meeting.
16. The project lost (its, it's) appeal after Mike quit.
17. I (ensure, assure) all print materials will be of high quality.
18. After you (ensure, assure) me, (assure, ensure) the others also.
19. (There, They're, Their) boat has left the dock.
20. We are (farther, further) along (than, then) we realize.
21. Say (its, it's) time to go, and we will.
22. If the bank will (loan, lend) you enough funds, will you buy the car?
23. My (principle, principal) and interest are due on the 1st of the month.
24. That company does all training on (sight, site).
25. Did the officer (site, cite) you for the violation?
26. When you document your sources, how do you (site, cite) a website?
27. We all try to live by our (principals, principles).

Note: See page 229 for the key to this activity.

Gender-Neutral Language

Gender-neutral language relates to word choice. During the past few decades, English vocabulary has dropped many of its sexist references.

Sexist references contribute to limiting a person's career choices. For example, men were not as likely to be enthusiastic about becoming *beauticians*, and women did not feel compelled to become *firemen*. However, now that terms such as *stylist* and *firefighter* are commonly used, both men and women experience more career options. Your writing, your speaking, and hopefully your thinking should reflect these changes. Here are a few examples. *Can you think of others?*

Sexist	Gender Neutral	Sexist	Gender Neutral
policeman	police officer	salesman	sales representative
waiter/waitress	food server	TV anchorman	news anchor
stewardess	flight attendant	mankind	humanity
mailman	postal worker	chairman	chair or chairperson

The change in language opens doors of opportunity because it opens people's minds to possibilities.

Unbiased Language

Word choices present a picture, setting a tone. For the sake of accuracy and diversity, choose words that eliminate bias from your writing and your speech. The *NASW Press Guidelines for Describing People* (2014) include the following points:

- Seek and use the preference of the people you write about.

- Be specific about age, race, and culture; for example, *Cuban Americans, Mexican Americans,* and *Puerto Ricans* is preferable to *Hispanics*.

- Describe people in the positive by stating what they are instead of what they are not.

- Avoid using terms that label people; for example, refer to people as *people*, not as objects, using a phrase such as *people with disabilities* rather than *the disabled*.

- Do not specify sex unless it is a variable or it is essential to the discussion.

For a thorough discussion, see the *NASW Press Guidelines for Describing People;* go to **https://www.naswpress.org/authors/guidelines/o8c-tools.html**.

Activity 8.2

Gender-Neutral and Unbiased Language

Instructions: For the outdated and biased words and phrases below, provide a revised or alternate term.

Outdated	Revised or Alternative
Policeman	
Waiter/waitress	
Fireman	
Stewardess	
Mailman	
Salesman	
TV anchorman	
Mankind	
Chairman	
Housewife	
Man a project	

Biased Language	
Schizophrenics	
Challenged	
Wheelchair-bound	
AIDS victims	
High-risk groups	
Nonwhite	
Minority	
Blacks	
Senior citizen or oldster	

Labels

The elderly or the aged   _____

The disabled or the handicapped   _____

The lower class   _____

The upper class   _____

The blind   _____

The hearing impaired   _____

Hispanic is a term that is sometimes used to represent which specific cultural groups?

_____

_____

What other outdated language, biased language, or labels have you encountered?

_____

_____

Note: See page 230 – 231 for the key to this activity.

Posttest

Instructions: In the sentences below, cross out any words that are used incorrectly, and write in the correct word above it or to the right of the sentence.

1. The affect of their decision is not yet known.

2. If its alright, I'll contact the manager directly.

3. We can meet everyday until we find a solution.

4. Bob would rather chair a meeting then host a dinner party.

5. When you pay off your principle early, you save on your interest.

6. My professor gave me good advise about my master's paper.

7. Take the time to ensure your clients that the change will support them.

8. Its been a challenging day, but things are getting better.

9. We are going their for lunch today.

10. On a daily basis, George travels further than I do.

11. Sam don't know who to trust with this situation.

12. Chuck assured delivery by the due date.

13. When you have alot of work, plan your time wisely.

14. Starting the meeting late was my ideal, not Jan's.

15. Try and create a positive tone from the beginning of the meeting.

Note: See page 231 for the key to this posttest.

Reference

National Association of Social Workers [NASW]. (2014). *NASW Press Guidelines for Describing People*. Retrieved from https://www.naswpress.org/authors/guidelines/08c-tools.html

Notes

9

Avoid Writing Traps

When writers are unsure of a convention, some tend to overuse it. For example, many writers are naïve about capitalization. Instead of respecting the basics and staying safe, they capitalize words almost randomly. Unsure writers do the same with possessives—an apostrophe is added haphazardly to words that end in an −s.

This workshop covers the following writing traps:

- Plurals and Possessives
- Capitalization

Unless you know for sure that a word should be capitalized, leave the word in lower case. To make capitalization decisions easier, learn a few simple rules, starting with the following:

When in doubt, do *not* capitalize.

In English, the *s* causes more problems than any other letter. Along with learning more about the *s*, you also learn how to use the apostrophe with possessives.

The Plan

1. Take the **pretest on** page 120.

2. Complete the **Workshop 9 Inventory** on page 120.

3. Review **Part 1: Plurals and Possessives** and complete all activities (Activity 9.1 through 9.4).

4. Review **Part 2: Capitalization**, and complete all activities (Activity 9.5 and 9.6).

5. Take the **posttest** on page 132; compare pretest and posttest results.

6. To further refine your skills, complete exercises as needed in Chapter 21, "Capitalization and Number Usage and Chapter 22, "Question Marks, Apostrophes, and Hyphens" in *The Writer's Handbook: A Guide for Social Workers* (2014).

Pretest

Instructions: Correct the errors in the following sentences.

1. Ms. Amanda Wittfield, Director of our company, will attend the meeting.
2. The womens' comments were not taken as they were meant.
3. Paul's and Mary's file was in the wrong cabinet.
4. You can ask Trent Olsen, the new Vice President of Marketing.
5. Our agencys' mission is to assist young people.
6. Send me a copy of your new book, *Finding A Job In 30 Days.*
7. Her assistants response was that he could not do the work.
8. The men and women responses were recorded by the assistant.
9. The speakers remark sparked the audience laughter.
10. Its all in a days work!

Workshop 9 Inventory

Instructions: Answer the questions below.

1. Capitalize common nouns that sound proper.   T/F
2. Always capitalize a person's official job title.   T/F
3. When a regular noun is plural and possessive, place the apostrophe after the *s*.   T/F
4. Capitalize business titles only when they immediately precede a name.   T/F
5. Proper nouns are always capitalized, but proper adjectives are not.   T/F
6. For irregular plural possessives, add an apostrophe plus *s*.   T/F
7. To understand capitalization, you must know the difference between a common noun and a proper noun.   T/F

Note: See page 232 for the keys to the pretest and inventory above.

PART 1: PLURALS AND POSSESSIVES

In this section, you learn about singular and plural possessives with regular and irregular nouns. Let's start by briefly reviewing nouns, as only nouns can be possessed.

Nouns as Possessions

Nouns and pronouns can show possession or ownership of other nouns. At times, it can be tricky to identify a possessive because some nouns are abstract, such as *belief* or *hope*.

The easiest way to determine whether a word is a noun is to place the word *the* in front of it. If the phrase sounds complete, the word is probably a noun, **for example:**

the idea	the thought	the color	the glare

When two nouns appear together, check to see if the first noun possesses the second one: Does the first noun need an apostrophe and *s* to show possession? **For example:**

Incorrect:	Bobs arrival	the windows display	the rooms color
Correct:	Bob's arrival	the window's display	the room's color

Singular Possessives

To form the possessive of a singular noun that does not end in *s,* add an apostrophe and *s ('s).* Here are some examples:

Singular Noun	**Singular Possessive**
book	book's cover
manager	manager's responsibilities
friend	friend's advice

When you are in doubt if a noun is showing possession, see if you can change the word order using the word *of,* for example "the day's end" becomes *the end of the day.*

the end of the meeting	the meeting's end
the beginning of the session	the session's beginning
the force of the wind	the wind's force

Activity 9.1

Possession and Word Order

Instructions: Change the following to the possessive form.

Example: the permission of the owner   the owner's permission

1. the friends of my brother   _____
2. the cover of the book   _____
3. the end of the day   _____
4. the influence of the team leader _____
5. the leaders of our nation   _____
6. the advice of my professor   _____
7. the reports of the agency   _____
8. the success of our team   _____
9. the color of the file   _____
10. the work of one day   _____

Note: See page 232 for the key to this activity.

Singular Nouns Ending in S

To form the possessive of a singular noun that ends in *s*, add an apostrophe alone or add an apostrophe plus an *s ('s)*. Follow these guidelines:

- If a new syllable is formed in the pronunciation of the possessive, add an apostrophe plus *s*, as in the following:

    the witness's answer   the hostess's guest list   the actress's role

- If the addition of an extra syllable would make the word challenging to pronounce, add only the apostrophe, as in the following:

    Mr. Jones' (or Jones's) meeting   for goodness' sake

When the singular form of a noun already ends in *s*, make the noun plural by adding *es* to the singular. Then form the possessive by adding an apostrophe. For example:

Singular	Singular Possessive	Plural	Plural Possessive
business	business's owner	businesses	businesses' owners
virus	virus's origination	viruses	viruses' originations

For last names (surnames) that end in *s, x, ch, sh,* or *z,* add *es* to form the plural. Then form the plural by adding an apostrophe, as in the following:

Singular	Singular Possessive	Plural	Plural Possessive
Fox	Mr. Fox's car	the Foxes	the Foxes' family reunion
Banks	Mary Banks' schedule	the Bankses	the Bankses' get together

Regular Plural Possessives

To form the possessive of a regular plural noun (a plural noun ending in *s* or *es*), add an apostrophe after the *s (s'):* make the noun plural *before* you make it possessive.

Singular Possessive	Plural Possessive (Count Nouns)
the owner's address	a few owners' addresses
our manager's decision	all of the managers' decisions
a client's question	many clients' questions

Notice in the above that when the possessive noun is plural, the object it modifies also becomes plural; these are *count nouns*. However, some nouns come *en masse* and are called *noncount nouns* because they cannot be counted. Examples include *paint* or *cake* or *food*. Other examples of noncount nouns are *honor, integrity,* and *humor.*

Singular Possessive	Plural Possessive (Noncount Nouns)
a person's integrity	many persons' integrity
a friend's help	our friends' help

Irregular Plural Possessives

To form the possessive of an irregular plural noun, change the singular form of the noun to the plural form and then add an apostrophe and *s (children's).*

Singular Possessive	Plural Possessive
a child's toy	the children's toys
one woman's theory	many women's theories
one man's idea	many men's ideas
a teenager's suggestion	several teenagers' suggestions
a woman's right	women's rights

Activity 9.2

Singular and Plural Possessives

Instructions: Turn the following nouns into singular possessives and then plural possessives.

For example:	Singular Possessive	Plural Possessive
sister	my <u>sister's</u> schedule	my two <u>sisters'</u> schedules

1. supervisor   my _____ office   both_____offices

2. teacher   this _____ table   these _____ tables

3. year   this _____schedule   both _____ schedules

4. assistant   my _____ laptop   our _____ laptops

5. student   the _____ speech   two _____ speeches

6. letter   a _____ address   these _____ addresses

7. client   the _____ needs   all _____ needs

8. child   the _____ file   both _____files

9. social worker   a _____ plan   two _____ plans

10. judge   a _____ ruling   many _____rulings

11. person   a _____ integrity   several _____integrity

12. woman   a _____ idea   many _____ideas

Note: See page 233 for the key to this activity.

Academic Degrees—Showing Possession

Use an apostrophe to show possession when referring to academic degrees in general terms:

bachelor's degree   master's degree   doctor's degree

However, academic degrees that are specific would not show possession:

master of science   bachelor of arts   doctorate

Note: For capitalization of degrees as well as course names and subjects, see pages 127 – 128.

Group Words

With group words or compound nouns, add the apostrophe and the *s* to the last term:

> the Queen of England's duties   her mother-in-law's address

To make a compound noun plural, add the s to the base word and the possessive ending to the last term. However, the preferred way is to change the word order, **for example:**

Awkward: their mothers-in-law's addresses

Preferred: the addresses of their mothers-in-law

Nouns in Series

When two nouns share joint possession, add the apostrophe only to the last noun. When there is individual possession, add the apostrophe to both nouns, **for example:**

Joint Ownership	**Individual Ownership**
Mitch and Teddy's mother	Mitch's and Teddy's houses
Margaret and Bill's project	Margaret's and Bill's projects

Abbreviations

To make an abbreviation plural, simply add an *s,* **for example**:

> three DVDs   blue M&Ms   five VCRs

To make an abbreviation possessive, add an apostrophe and *s,* **for example:**

> ABC's newscast   the CSWE's guidelines   BPD's conference

Possessives Standing Alone

At times, a writer will compare two nouns that are showing possession but leave off the item being possessed after the second noun. Note that the second noun also shows possession.

> Barb's remark was similar to George's (remark).
>
> We will meet in Alex's office, not Miko's (office).
>
> Michele is working on her master's (degree).

Activity 9.3

Possessives Standing Alone

Instructions: Look for possessives and make corrections where necessary.

Incorrect: Toby's input was more helpful than Dugan.

Corrected: Toby's input was more helpful than *Dugan's (input)*.

1. Ambras and Lucias instructor refuses to let them work together.
2. Either Alexi's report or Basma will persuade the judge.
3. Milton suggested that we go to Ditkas for the meeting.
4. My brother-in-laws attorneys opened their office last week.
5. Chandras and her partners office needs to be remodeled.

Activity 9.4

Possessive Review

Instructions: Correct errors in possessives *as well as other errors in grammar.*

1. The report was given at last weeks meeting.
2. The departments duties were change dramatically.
3. When she spoke, everyone was aware it was Bobs error.
4. The supervisor wanted to change the meetings location.
5. The directors assistant was rude.
6. A weeks time had pass before we noticed the change.
7. The manager spoke highly of both Jim and Robins reports.
8. There is few people who know the reports real recommendation.
9. Alice remark was very similar to George.
10. When she ask to many question, her teams attitude change.
11. The reports was in Mr. Jones office.
12. When we arrived, we looked for Joe and Margie report.

Note: See page 233 for the keys to the above activities.

PART 2: CAPITALIZATION

In other words, unless you know for sure that a word should be capitalized, leave the word in lower case. Here are the two major categories of words that should be capitalized:

- Proper nouns
- First words of sentences, poems, direct quotations, complimentary closings, and statements following a colon.

Note: Also capitalize the first word of a complete sentence that follows a word of instruction or caution, such as *Note* or *Caution* (as illustrated here).

Proper Nouns and Common Nouns

To avoid making capitalization errors, know the difference between proper nouns and common nouns. Here are some examples:

Proper Noun	Common Noun
John Wilson	name, person, friend, business associate
Wilson Corporation	company, corporation, business
New York	state, city, country
Federal Government	federal employees, federal guidelines, and so on

Words derived from proper nouns become proper adjectives and are capitalized:

Proper Noun	Derivative or Proper Adjective
England	English language
Spain	Spanish 101
Italy	Italian cookware
French	French class

Most words are common nouns, even academic disciplines, for example:

sociology   social work   psychology   biology

When used as part of a title, such as course names, they become proper nouns:

Sociology 101   Psychology 225

Human Behavior and Social Work, Social Work 435

The personal pronoun *I* is a proper noun and should *always* be capitalized:

Incorrect: A friend asked me if i could help, so i said that i would.

Corrected: A friend asked if I could help, so I said that I would.

Academic Degrees and Capitalization

When referring to academic degrees in general terms, do not capitalize them:

bachelor's degree	master's degree	doctor's degree
master of science	bachelor of arts	bachelor's in social work

When using the full name of a degree, capitalize it:

Bachelor of Arts in Sociology   Master of Science in Social Work

When the name of the degree follows a personal name, capitalize it whether it is written in full or abbreviated. When a degree is abbreviated, you can use periods or not, but be consistent:

Jane Addams, Bachelor of Social Work   Jane Addams, BSW

Jack E. Robinson, M.S.W.   Jack E. Robinson, BSW, MSW

Organizational Titles and Terms

Most people believe that their job title is a proper noun, but professional titles are *not* proper nouns. Here are some rules to follow:

- Capitalize a professional title when it precedes the name.
- Do not capitalize a professional title when it follows the name.
- Capitalize organizational terms in your own company (but not necessarily other companies), such as the names of departments and committees.

Incorrect: John Smith, Vice President, will meet with us.

Corrected: John Smith, vice president, will meet with us.

Corrected: Vice President John Smith will meet with us.

The titles of high government officials are capitalized, for example:

The President had a meeting in the West Wing of the White House.

Hyphenated Terms

Here are guidelines for capitalizing hyphenated terms.

- Capitalize parts of the hyphenated word that are proper nouns, **for example**:

  If I receive your information by mid-December, you will qualify for the training.

- Capitalize each word of a hyphenated term used in a title (except short prepositions and conjunctions, as previously noted), **for example**:

  Up-to-Date Reports   Long-Term Outlook   E-Mail Guidelines

Activity 9.5

Capitalization Review

Instructions: Correct errors in possessives *as well as other errors in grammar.*

1. The director of social services, Phillip James, called the client.
2. Have you taken enough english and math to meet the requirements?
3. The federal government employs thousands of people.
4. Many federal employees appreciate that benefit.
5. Will professor Davis hold a make up session?
6. Are you majoring in social work? If so, take social work 421 next semester.
7. Note: all proposals are due by the first of the month.
8. You can ask your professor about the project; would that be professor Martinez?
9. The director of our agency said, "we are due for important change."
10. Did professor Ford attend the convention?
11. We love to visit european cities when we travel.
12. Yesterday the director of social services, Julia McGregor, revealed her plans.
13. Yesterday director of social services Julia McGregor revealed her plans.
14. Yesterday Julia McGregor, director of social services, revealed her plans.
15. Our social worker, Sylvia Hines, is taking the case.
16. The counselor asked, "would you like another copy of nasws code of ethics?"
17. When you receive your bachelors degree, will it be a bachelor of science in social work?
18. If you can, work on your masters degree, get a master of science in social work.

Note: See page 234 for the key to this activity.

Articles, Conjunctions, and Prepositions in Titles

Not every word of a title is capitalized, and the types of words in question are articles, conjunctions, and prepositions. Here's what to look for:

Articles:	the, a, an
Conjunctions:	and, but, or, for, nor
Prepositions:	to, at, in, from, among, over, and so on

Here are rules about capitalizing articles, conjunctions, and prepositions:

1. Capitalize any of these words when it is the first word of a title or subtitle.

2. Capitalize a preposition when it is the first or last word of a title or subtitle.

Sources vary about the capitalization of prepositions in other positions in a title. For example, though some sources require prepositions to remain in lower case even when they consist of five or more letters, *APA requires the following*:

- Prepositions of *three or fewer letters* must be in *lower case*.

- Prepositions of *four or more letters* must be *capitalized*. (In fact, any word that has four or more letters would be capitalized in APA style.)

Here are some examples:

The University of Chicago

Patient Protection and Affordable Care Act

Tuesdays With Morrie (APA style)

Tuesdays with Morrie (most styles other than APA)

APA Style: Title Case and Sentence Case

For presenting titles, APA style uses two different types of capitalization styles, *title case* and *sentence case.*

- For *title case*, type titles in upper and lower case letters, following the basic guidelines for capitalization presented in this chapter. For example, capitalize all words in the title except for articles, coordinating conjunctions, and prepositions of three letters or fewer. Use title case for the following:
  - The title of your paper
  - The title of a book, article, or chapter *within the text of your paper*

- For *sentence case*, capitalize the first word of the title and the first word following a colon (the subtitle) as well as proper nouns and proper adjectives; all other words are typed in lower case. Use sentence case as follows:
  - The titles of books, articles, or websites (but not the title of the publisher or a journal) *with references listed on the reference page*

For example:

In text: *Tuesdays With Morrie: An Old Man, a Young Man, and Life's Greatest Lesson*
Reference: *Tuesdays with Morrie: An old man, a young man, and life's greatest lesson*

In text: *The Writer's Handbook: A Guide for Social Workers*
Reference: *The writer's handbook: A guide for social workers*

Activity 9.6

Capitalizing Book and Article Titles in APA Style

Instructions: For the following, show how the title would be displayed in APA style first as an in-text reference and then as a formal reference on the reference page.

1. **Book Title:** Research with Human Subjects

    In text:

    Reference:

2. **Book title:** Helping Skills for Social Workers

    In text:

    Reference:

3. **Article title:** The Implementation of the Patient Protection and Affordable Care Act

    In text:

    Reference:

4. **Article title:** Projects: A Key to Student Learning

    In text:

    Reference:

5. Website title: Patient Protection and Affordable Care Act

In text:

Reference: Patient Protection and Affordable Care Act

6. Website title: Strengthening Your Writing Skills: An Essential Task for Social Workers

In text:

Reference:

Note: See page 234 – 235 for the key to the above activity.

Now that you have improved your skills, take the posttest and compare the results with your pretest.

Posttest

Instructions: Correct the errors in the following sentences.

1. Amanda will complete her Bachelors Degree in Social Work this fall.

2. The childrens' toys were scattered around the play room.

3. I have taken several classes in social work this year.

4. My favorite class was writing in the field, social work 270.

5. The professor of the class is Director of Child Services.

6. He recommended reading the book How To Find A Job In 30 Day's.

7. When you receive your Masters in Social Work, you can put MSW after your name.

8. Mary received her bachelors degree last year and is now working on her masters.

9. Every time that i tried to assist the client, she refused my help.

10. Its all in a days work!

Note: See page 235 for the key to this posttest.

Notes

10

Write Effective Grants and Proposals

Writing an effective grant or a proposal can feel exhilarating: you identify a serious need, describe how to solve it, and develop an argument that demonstrates that you and your agency or organization are the best choice to fulfill the need. At the same time, writing a grant or proposal is challenging and, at times, the process can feel intimidating.

- A *proposal* is a plan that offers a solution to a problem, persuading stakeholders to do something, whether it is to adopt a new idea, service, or product.

- A *grant*—or *grant proposal*—is a request for funding for a specific project that you initiate, usually presented to an organization or agency that would support the project's mission.

As a form of persuasive writing, grant writing involves planning and research. You are making an argument that is supported by data and evidence. Though you may spend six months writing a grant proposal, your reviewers may spend only minutes determining whether to fund it. At times, your job may depend on getting your grant proposal funded.

Let's get started by reviewing the basics of grant proposals and then, later in the chapter, review some elements of basic proposals.

Grant Proposals

From conception to implementation, writing and maintaining a grant is a process. Here are parts that you will need to develop:

1. Statement of Need
2. Target Population
3. Goals and Objectives
4. Program Design and Project Activities
5. Organization and Staffing (including collaboration with other individuals, groups, and private or governmental agencies)

6. Capacity / Resources
7. Evaluation
8. Sustainability, *if applicable*

In addition, if your grant is funded, you will be required to report outcomes.

Request for Proposal (RFP)

When funding organizations have specific needs, they may release a public announce-ment in the form of a *request for proposal* (RFP) or *request for application* (RFA).

- An RFP establishes the scope of the intended project and alerts interested parties that the funding organization is soliciting competitive bids and formal proposals.

- An RFA announces that grant funding is available so that interested agencies become aware of the opportunity as well as submission requirements, expectations, and guidelines for applying.

Funding organizations use RFPs, in part, so that respondents provide complete information and use a uniform format, facilitating comparison and evaluation. Before submitting—*or even starting*—a formal proposal, learn the funding organization's requirements. State and federal governments along with not-for-profit foundations have the most complicated guidelines for grants and proposals.

Here's a strategy for reviewing an RFP or an RFA. As you go through it, use a highlighter to mark information to find later. Start by identifying the application due date—*can you meet it?* Work backwards from the due date to create a time-line. Be sure to give yourself a few extra days for equipment failure, other unforeseen events, and shipping.

- Read the eligibility criteria
  - *Are you eligible to apply?*
  - *Are there geographic or other types of restrictions?*
- Read the project exclusion criteria (common exclusions: conference, salaries)
- Read the table of contents
- See formatting (page limit, margins, font), and submission method instructions
- Identify the contact person

Formal Proposals

Formal proposals involve considerable research and development. To be successful, the writer (or writers) must understand the problem along with evidence-based solutions. The writer must also use the formal structure and guidelines that the funding organization requires.

Your proposal must convince the reader of the following:

- That a problem exists and needs to be solved.
- That you and/or your agency are the best choice to solve the problem.
- That your approach—your plan—is the most effective.
- That your costs are competitive and justified.

Proposal format varies among funding organizations. An individual or committee may evaluate your proposal along with many others; consistency in format is essential so that evaluators can see if the proposal is complete and compare it with others.

- If a proposal does not follow the prescribed format exactly, it may be returned without being read.
- Evaluators may make their decision within the first moments of reviewing a grant, using the remainder of their time to validate their initial opinion.

Ask your peers to review your grant thoroughly. Also format it meticulously, ensuring that *the why* is presented effectively before developing *the how*. Below is the format that The Foundation Center recommends.

Table 10.1. The Foundation Center – Components of a Proposal (2015)

Part	Description	Length
Executive Summary:	A summary of the entire proposal.	1 page
Statement of Need:	A description of why the proposal is necessary.	2 pages
Project Description	How the program will be implemented and evaluated.	3 pages
Budget:	Financial description of the project and explanation.	1 page
Organization Information:	History and governing structure of the nonprofit; its primary activities, audiences, and services.	1 page
Conclusion	Summary of the proposal's main points	2 paragraphs

Basic Parts of a Proposal

Proposal requirements vary somewhat from organization to organization, though most proposals contain the following parts.

Statement of Need

Purpose: Start with a short statement connecting your agency to the needs of the potential recipients of the services that the grant would provide. Briefly state information about the need to solve the problem; relate confidence in developing a comprehensive or innovative solution.

Background: Give a brief history of the problem, providing data that supports the problem. Give details about individual objectives the proposal will address. Include enough information so that the reader becomes motivated to have you solve the problem. *In short, why should they fund your proposal?*

Project Description

Objectives: State what you will accomplish by writing individual objectives for major parts of the project.

Plan, methods, and schedule: Discuss the details of how you will achieve your purpose and objectives; identify the methods you will use and the order in which you will use them. State how long the activities will take and give dates, if applicable. For example, "phase one," "phase two," and so on.

Results: Summarize the expected outcomes that implementing your proposal will achieve.

Organization Information

Your agency: Include relevant information about your organization's history, management structure, clients, and services. Include information about community partnerships with organizations who support your grant.

Staffing and Credentials: Provide the names and credentials for those who will implement the proposal. (For shorter letter proposals, present this information in a less formal way.)

Budget	Include a detailed breakdown of the costs. Justify any costs that may seem extraordinary.
Evaluation	Explain how you will measure results. Indicate how you (and the funder) will know if you achieve the objectives?
Authorization	Include an authorization statement for the funder along with a signature line. (In shorter, less formal proposals, the authorization statement is often omitted.)

A formal proposal is a contract, so expect to be held responsible for any service you indicate that you can provide and at the cost that you list. Thus, you may want to indicate the time frame during which the proposal is effective. For example:

The costs quoted in this proposal are valid until the end of this year.

Proposals represent partnerships. You are linking your skills with others to solve a problem that may affect people you have never met. Hence, early in the process, , if you are writing a proposal for an agency, be sure you understand the aspect of the agency that would provide the services and develop an understanding of the people they intend to serve through the grant.

Community Relationships

Writing proposals includes listening to the needs of the agency and the people who will be impacted by the programs supported by the funds and then customizing solutions to this particular population. Thus, proposals extend from the needs data your agency has gathered (not from what *you think* the needs are). These needs must be demonstrated through data, information that supports the concerns identified by the agency and community.

In addition, the proposed project is often part of a larger organizational process that helps the organization fulfill its mission. For example, assume that you are working for an agency that provides services to teens in the neighborhood. Many of their parents are working when school closes at the end of the day. Your agency has gathered data that shows the teens are most likely to get in trouble between the time school ends and their parents return home, around 6 p.m. Therefore, your agency is seeking funds for an afterschool program that would provide tutoring, recreational activities, and snacks to teens.

A writer or task group needs to tailor *every detail* to the potential recipients of the services whom the grant or proposal will support.

Collaboration is a key to successful grants. Take the following steps in developing a base for your proposals:

1. Research the philosophies, cultures, and mission of the potential service recipients.
2. If possible and appropriate, establish an honest dialog with the decision-makers and stakeholders in the community. (In the example of the afterschool program, key stakeholders would include the teens, parents, teachers, law enforcement, and probation.)

Obviously some situations do not allow direct contact with prospective clients; but when you can meet with potential service recipients, doing so is your most important work. By clarifying needs, you have the groundwork for defining your purposes, methods, and outcomes.

Cover Letter

Many grants are now submitted online, and a cover letter is generally not part of that process. However, when submitting hard copy grants, include a cover letter summarizing main points of the grant (taken from the executive summary and statement of need).

The cover letter gives evaluators their first impression, so make sure it is well written, beautifully formatted and accurate. However, the cover letter does not need to contain *new* information; you can use direct statements from the proposal or executive summary. By summarizing highlights from the proposal, the letter prepares the reader for the language and ideas that the proposal contains.

Letter Proposal

At times, funding organizations do not require formal proposals. For example, when a letter proposal is requested, the funder may be asking for details in writing to grant approval or finalize authorization. Your proposal is basically a contract for the services you will provide.

When this is the case, a two-page letter proposal will generally suffice. The letter proposal contains most of the same information that a longer, formal proposal contains. Though all proposals need to be tailored to the specific audience, here are guidelines for a two-page letter proposal:

Statement of Need

Start with a short statement connecting your agency's needs with your expertise. Once again, *why should they hire you?*

Description of Project

Objectives	State what you will accomplish by writing objectives for major parts of the project.
Plan and Schedule	Discuss only important details of your plan. Identify each phase of the proposal and give dates for availability, if applicable. If feasible, give your client options.
Results / Evaluation	State the results your proposal will accomplish and how you will measure them.
Budget	Include a detailed breakdown of the costs. If you have given options, make sure the costs for each option are clear.

Proposal Details

An agency task group may write a proposal for various reasons: for example, to persuade members of its own organization to make changes or to persuade external organizations to sponsor a program. One common type of proposal is to request funds from a not-for-profit foundation or government agency to implement a project.

Here are the basics of proposal writing:

- Establishing that a problem exists and that you are the best one to solve it.
- Knowing who the key stakeholders are what they are seeking.
- Incorporating into your plan solutions tailored to your key stakeholders.

When you clarify the problem, provide evidence, such as statistics. For example, in a south side neighborhood, 40 percent of the juvenile arrests were made during weekdays between 2:30 p.m. and 6:30 p.m. Your agency already provides services to these teens. You have a support letter from the principal of the school who has agreed to allow your agency staff to use the gym for the afterschool program. She has also committed assistance from the school staff who are providing an afterschool program for younger teens who meet in a different building. The principal's letter also stated that the older teens have been hanging around the afterschool program and have shown interest in afterschool activities.

Different types of proposals have different types of requirements, some more rigid than others. Define the scope of your proposal:

- What are your funder's requirements? Has your funder published a formal RFP that outlines their needs?

- Does your proposal need to include every element of a formal proposal or the RFP?

- Can your proposal be a short letter or memo that addresses only a few questions?

Before you begin working on your proposal, take an honest inventory:

1. What are the eligibility criteria—do you meet them?

2. What is the due date—can you do it in time?

3. What are the formatting requirements and submission method?

What Is Your Vision?   Start the process by identifying a need that you have a passion for addressing. Though "passion" makes a strong statement, that is the kind of energy needed to sustain you through the research, planning, and implementation of the project. If an issue does not merit your passion, is it worth pursuing?

- How can you make a difference?

- What issues or needs tug at your heartstrings?

- What is your *mission*? What is your *vision*?

What Is Your Project?   Describe your project in detail, answering the six journalist's questions: *who, what, when, where, why,* and *how.* Here is an overview of the questions you will answer:

- **Who:**   Who is your target population?

    Who will do the work?

    What is the history of your agency?

    Also, who are the key stakeholders of the organization to which you are submitting your grant and what do they value?

- **What:**   What is your project design?

- **When:**   What is your timeline?

- **Where:**   Where is the program site?

- **Why:**   Why is your project important?
- **How:**   What are your goals and objectives?

Who Will Do the Work?   To describe your agency and staff in detail, answer the following questions:

- What is the history of your agency? What are its accomplishments?
- What is the structure of your agency?
- What are the qualifications of your supervisory staff?
- What are the credentials and skills of the project staff?

Also, are you writing your grant alone or will you work with a team of colleagues or task group? Will community collaborators work with you on this project?

- What is a formal description of the agencies and collaborators?
- Why are they interested?
- What type of support (staff, funding, space) will they contribute?

Next, review the cover letter and grant proposal on pages 144 – 150.

The most important part of your proposal, or any persuasive writing, is *the why*:

Readers connect to your proposal through *the why*, which puts every other piece of your proposal in context. If readers do not feel invested in *the why*, *the how* quickly becomes irrelevant: *providing persuasive evidence is essential.*

Figure 10.2. Cover Letter for Grant Proposal

August 26, 2015

Mr. Charles C. Yanuvich, Chairman
The Foundation
444 Wacker Drive, Suite 2202
Chicago, IL 60601

Dear Mr. Yanuvich:

I am pleased to present Family Shelter Service's proposal to the Foundation. We are honored by your past commitment to our agency and hope to enter into another successful partnership with The Foundation to provide essential services to families escaping violence. We are requesting $10,000 in general operating support on behalf of approximately 2,000 women and children.

Our mission aligns perfectly with the philosophy of The Foundation. The vision to "expand mankind's horizons" aligns with our own mission to help victims of domestic violence to realize their potential. When children are safe, they are free to grow. When women can see themselves as viable leaders of their families and know that they no longer have to live in fear, they feel empowered. Every day our counselors see these transformations take place.

The success of our work depends on the support of informed and committed friends. We are deeply grateful that the Foundation has recognized the importance of our residential, counseling and advocacy programs for victims of domestic violence. We hope to re-engage that support on behalf of families who often have nowhere else to turn in their time of crisis.

Sincerely,

Shaheen Ahmed
Grant Coordinator

Figure 10.3. Grant Proposal

Proposal for the Period July 1, 2015-June 30, 2016

Purpose of Grant

We are pleased to submit Family Shelter Service's proposal for the period July 1, 2015, through June 30, 2016. We are requesting $10,000 for general operating funds. We are honored to have the past partnership of the Foundation and hope to re-engage your support on behalf of women and children escaping situations of violence.

Proposal Summary

Family Shelter Service's mission is to address the issue of domestic violence by providing services to victims of domestic violence through our three core programs: residential, counseling, and community advocacy. Our services include: safe, emergency housing which is available 24 hours a day, 365 days a year; two intermediate housing facilities for clients ready for independent living; individual, group, and family counseling; case management; employment services; court and victim advocacy; a 24-hour crisis hotline and a counseling program specifically designed for children. 88% of our clients are female; we also serve boys up to the age of 18 and male survivors of elder abuse. Services are available in English and in Spanish. Family Shelter also plays a vital role in raising community awareness through our PEACE project, providing education and engaging the community in a dialogue about this devastating societal issue.

Our overarching goal for each client is to move toward sustainable safety and self-sufficiency. Our outcomes measure the success rate at which our clients have acquired the tools (knowledge/skills gained or the development of new behaviors) that make this goal attainable.

Each residential client completes a departure survey. The survey includes questions about what types of aftercare services are of interest to the client as well as questions regarding the client's experiences in the program. Individual counseling clients are surveyed once a year and group-counseling clients are surveyed during the last group session. Over the course of the funding period, we anticipate the following outcomes for clients across all programs:

We expect 85% of our clients to report that:

- I know more ways to plan for my safety.
- I know more about community resources.
- I have a better understanding of domestic violence.

We expect 85% of mothers of children in our Children's Program to report that their children have learned non-violent ways to solve problems.

Outcome surveys have been modified for children and data are collected from our child clients at the same intervals as adults. Service providers meet with the parent or caretaker of all child clients before services begin, to get an idea of the immediate needs that led them to seek counseling. During this meeting, a developmental and behavior history is taken to get a fuller picture of the possible longer-standing areas of concern. The Trauma Symptom Checklist (TSCC) or the Trauma Symptom Checklist for Young Children (TSCYC) is given to all of our child clients ages 3-16 as a part of the intake process. These tools help us identify any critical areas of concern -- such as potential self-injury, suicidality, and a desire to harm others -- that may require immediate attention. These measures also let the provider know if a child has clinically significant scores on anxiety, depression, and post-traumatic stress scales.

Child-Parent Psychotherapy (CPP) is an intervention used for children from birth to age 5 who have experienced at least one traumatic event. If a child 5 or younger is referred to counseling, or if a parent is in need of parenting help, CPP may be offered, with the goal of supporting and strengthening the relationship between a child and his or her parent or caregiver. A service plan is developed within the first few sessions and focuses on restoring the child's sense of safety, attachment, and appropriate affect, along with helping the caregiver understand how a history of trauma may be affecting perceptions and interactions with the child so s/he can interact with the child in new, developmentally appropriate ways.

Program Update

Since our last submission to the Foundation, we have restructured our programs to more efficiently meet current need. The growth of our programs over our 39-year history has been catalyzed by the demand for services in the community. However, we realize that some of our programs are duplicated by other agencies in the county. We realized that we needed to conduct comprehensive appraisal of how integrated our services are, and whether or not they meet the changing needs of victims in the community. We must consider our services from the perspective of the client, who may have multiple program needs simultaneously and urgently. We have also extended ourselves to address the needs of clients who are no longer in the immediate stage of crisis, which has limited our capacity to provide a first-response effort to a larger number of victims in the community. In May 2014, we launched a process to evaluate whether our programs are directly meeting client needs in a timely and seamless way. Since that time, we have been in the process of reimagining our programs, with changes piloted in FY15 and to be completed in FY16.

First, we researched best practices and developed a vision of programs "from the ground up." We learned that there are three phases recommended for trauma treatment: Phase 1: safety; Phase 2: stabilization; Phase 3: longer-term healing and a greater connection between client and community. We have identified the first two phases as being the focus of our work at Family Shelter. Our new program structure will be a phase-based approach to healing that emphasizes safety and stabilization, that moves clients through a continuum of services, and that helps to prepare clients for longer-term services elsewhere in the community. Safety is our first priority and is addressed through programs such as our hotline, emergency shelter, and court and victim advocacy programs, which focus on identifying immediate needs, safety planning, and crisis management and support.

Phase 2 of our program services focuses on stabilization. Stabilizing services help clients to improve daily functioning, self-regulation, self-esteem, and self-care, as well as providing psycho-education on domestic violence. Clients begin to process their experiences, but focus much more on case management and skill-building. This is achieved through in-person emotional support, case management, Child-Parent Psychotherapy sessions, and group sessions. In this phase, clients who are interested in longer-term services can also prepare for this transition. Services such as time-limited individual sessions, family counseling, and drop-in or peer-led support groups prepare clients to make connections in the community and enter longer-term treatment programs if they so choose; however, our primary goals are for clients to be able to function well and feel safe in their day-to-day lives.

Next, we worked to identify the services we offer that are unique to the community and that are central to our new vision of programs. They are as follows: Hotline; First Responders to domestic violence incidents – Court/Victim Advocacy and Emergency Shelter; Teen Program; Child-Parent Psychotherapy for children aged 5 and under; prevention programming; and our Latino Program.

Once our core programs were identified, we worked to re-imagine ways to increase our responsiveness and efficiency in meeting client needs. The first and foremost need for domestic violence victims is safety. We need to have a nimble response to clients who are at immediate risk of harm. Our Hotline and Victim/Court Advocacy programs are part of our first response to victims, but we realized that we can optimize these programs by envisioning and implementing flexible programming that allows for fluid staffing across programs. For example, when a victim calls our hotline, we need to address their immediate safety. However, some clients do not have or cannot identify their immediate safety needs, but may need to talk to a counselor to process their experiences. We have begun to implement an assessment tool on the hotline that allows us to better identify those clients with the most immediate safety needs versus those who are relatively safe, but require assistance with stabilization.

For those clients with immediate safety needs, we want to offer a fast track to a suite of critical services, which may include emergency shelter, crisis counseling, and logistical help. In February 2015, we expanded our programming to offer a 24- to 48-hour in-person response for callers on the hotline who are in crisis and unable to wait for services.

This triage process on our hotline enables clients in immediate need of safety to be seen within a very short time frame by staff whose skill set matches the needs of the client. Since residential staff is accustomed to addressing the needs of clients in immediate crisis, we can use their expertise to provide a timely and effective response to hotline clients who need urgent help, fulfilling the "safety" area of client need. Clients calling our hotline may also have their concerns addressed by a member of the counseling staff via the triage process. This new model of programming meets client needs with appropriate services from qualified staff in a timely way.

We also know that, beyond our core programs, there are other agencies that own the expertise in issues relevant to victims of domestic violence, and that we can establish stronger partnerships that will be beneficial to our clients. We have begun to identify, build, and strengthen partnerships with community agencies that allow us to provide a wider range of services that address client safety or that support clients in the stabilization phase of services.

An example of this program change began in our Employment Readiness services in February of this year. Many of our clients need assistance with addressing their economic viability. Their work histories or education may have been interrupted; their abuser may have sabotaged their finances and/or credit rating. We have offered Employment Readiness services, including a Career Club, at Family Shelter's Downers Grove location for several years. However, we realized that there are many successful agencies specifically addressing this issue throughout the county, and we decided to research a potential partner that could increase our outreach into the community. Our research led us to the Community Career Center of South Naperville, with which we are now collaborating. Staff from the Center will be conducting daytime sessions of Career Club with one of our volunteers at our Downers Grove shelter and counseling facility. Family Shelter Service clients will have access to all of their services free of charge: the usual fee of $50 will be waived for our clients, whether they access the services of the Community Career Center at our site or at the Center's own South Naperville location. We will continue to offer evening sessions of Career Club at our location with our own staff and volunteers. In addition, our Director of Training will go to the Community Career Center location in Naperville and provide an on-site support group for clients of the Center who are domestic violence survivors.

Success story from Funding Year FY15

Funding from the Foundation was designated towards general operating support. We would like to share a success story from the funded year that demonstrates the breadth of our services to families escaping violence.

Inez is a 28-year old Latina woman and mother of three: Maria who is 13 years old, Alondra who is 9 years old, and Felipe who is 6 years old. Inez initially called our hotline and shared her traumatizing experiences of violence at home. Our hotline counselor assessed her need for immediate refuge and found a place for Inez and her children at our emergency residential shelter in Downers Grove. Inez is most comfortable in her first language, Spanish. The family attended our Moms & Kids group in Spanish, where Inez was able to connect with other women who have experienced domestic violence and share resources and information. Maria connected with other teens in our Teen Support Group; Alondra and Felipe made friends and were able to begin speaking about their anxieties. With parenting support services received, the mother-child bond between Inez and her three children was strengthened. Inez regained her confidence and was able to leave our residential program in the spring. She obtained full-time employment and rented her first apartment. The family was able to continue healing through ongoing services and the children learned non-violent conflict resolution skills.

Collaboration with Other Agencies

Family Shelter is a founding member of the Illinois Coalition Against Domestic Violence. Family Shelter Service is deeply invested in the work of the 18th Judicial Circuit Family Violence Coordinating Council (FVCC). Staff members participate regularly in several FVCC activities, including the Steering Committee and the Court & Law Enforcement, Education, Faith, Symposium, and Family Justice Center sub-committees. FSS staff also assists in planning the Council's annual symposium during Domestic Violence Awareness Month. FVCC meetings occur monthly or quarterly throughout the year and bring a variety of front-line service providers together to address issues related to domestic violence. Other participants in the local FVCC include members of the judiciary, the State's Attorney's Office, the Public Defender's Office, the Circuit Court Clerk's Office, the Department of Probation and Court Services, the Partner Abuse Intervention Program of DuPage County's Psychological Services, the DuPage County Family Center, the Sheriff's Department, Hamdard Center, DCFS, the DuPage County Health Department, and the DuPage Federation for Human Services Reform. Community members – including attorneys, educators, medical personnel, and law enforcement officers – are also regular participants.

Family Shelter's Victim/Court Advocacy Program is housed in the DuPage County Courthouse. As a result, our advocates communicate frequently with members of the judiciary, the State's Attorney's Office, and the Circuit Court Clerk's Office regarding system issues that impact clients. Family Shelter's Victim/Court Advocacy Program enjoys a long-standing partnership with local law enforcement through the DuPage County Domestic Violence Protocol. The Protocol mandates that officers in all 33 police jurisdictions who respond to a domestic violence incident must contact the FSS hotline by the end of their shift to make a report. Victim advocates then do outreach to the identified victim, providing information and referrals by mail and/or phone within hours of the incident. Family Shelter Service offers training opportunities to law enforcement, providing officer training a minimum of 3 to 5 times per year. Family Shelter's "Bathroom Project" connects us to health care providers throughout the county, many of which display our informational posters and hotline cards in their bathroom stalls, where victims can access them in privacy. FSS staff meets monthly with staff from Advocate Good Samaritan Hospital to collaborate on trainings and to improve screening for domestic violence throughout the hospital. FSS and Advocate Good Samaritan also offer an annual symposium; this year, we hosted nearly 121 professionals at this symposium. Family Shelter's Second-Stage Housing Coordinator works closely with local transitional housing providers, such as Catholic Charities, Bridge Communities, and Loretto House. She communicates frequently with case managers and attends monthly meetings to ensure that clients transition smoothly from shelter to transitional or independent housing.

We maintain relationships by participating in many community networking groups, such as: DuPage Federation for Human Services Reform, DCFS-LAN, Latino Services Provider Network, Take Back the Night/EVA Organizing Committee, Homeless Continuum of Care, DHS Community Quality Council, and the West Suburban Jobs Council, among others. We have ongoing networking agreements with Serenity House for substance abuse referrals, Literacy DuPage for ESL classes, and the Health Department for a visiting nurse in shelter. In FY16, we will be partnering with the Community Career Center of Naperville; CCC staff will provide job club services at our Downers Grove location, and FSS staff will provide domestic violence informational groups at the CCC offices. We continue to pursue collaborative relationships that enhance supports for our clients.

Conclusion

Our comprehensive programs address the complex and unique needs of victims of domestic violence, wherever they are on their journey towards safety. A woman seeking to build a safer life for herself and her children must confront seemingly overwhelming obstacles. Timely and informed support is critical to connect her to counseling services that address the trauma she and her children have experienced; case management to assist her in overcoming the logistical challenges that prevent her from realizing her long-term goals; expertise to help her navigate the judicial process to ensure legal protection for herself and her family. We know that it takes a collaborative effort to respond effectively to women and children affected by domestic abuse. We are grateful for the past support of the Foundation and hope to continue our successful partnership to ensure that women and children are met with the support and tools they need to build safer lives.

Letter of Inquiry

According to the Foundation Center (2015), "Many foundations now prefer that funding requests be submitted first in letter format instead of a full proposal. Others are using preliminary letters of inquiry to determine if they have an interest in a project before accepting a full proposal" (para. 1).

Therefore, your contact with a funding organization may be a letter of inquiry. You would target funding organizations that have shown an interest in similar projects.

Start by describing the program, the institution, and the issue. Here are the questions that you will answer as you develop your letter of inquiry:

- What are the needs or the problems to be solved?
- Who will benefit and how?
- What is the scope and methodology of your project?
- What is the time required for completion?
- What institutional comments do you need?
- Do you need special capabilities or equipment to ensure the project's success?

Keep your letter to 3 pages or less, and consider breaking your letter into the following sections:

- Introduction
- Agency description
- Statement of need
- Methodology
- Other funding sources and collaboration
- Final summary

Though you generally do not need to include budget information unless they ask for it, mention if you already have some financial support for the project.

To see sample letters, do a search on "letters of inquiry."

Executive Summary

An executive summary is more than a summary: Many reviewers will make up their minds within the first few moments of beginning their review of the summary.

Therefore, your executive summary must persuade the reader that your proposal has enough merit to warrant funding your project. To keep that aim in sight, think of your executive summary as a marketing tool.

As a social work professional, you may not be as versed in "selling" your services as you are in providing them. For example, for some majors, such as business, marketing is an important part of the curriculum. Though you may not have a formal background in marketing, understand that if a funding organization cannot be persuaded and does not "buy into" the merit of your proposal, you will not be funded.

An executive summary is the doorway to the rest of the document. Write your executive summary so that it informs and influences the reader, assuming that the full proposal may not even be read.

- Think of your executive summary as a stand-alone document.
- Keep your executive summary to 5 to 10 percent of your entire document.
- Use *evidence* to develop your argument.
- Define the problem in a clear and understandable way, adapting the language for your audience.
- Provide a tangible, achievable solution for the problem.
- Keep your paragraphs short and concise.
- Break your document into sections, using headings so that key parts are accessible
- Format professionally: create a document that is inviting *at a glance*.

Writing is persuasive when it is clear, concise, reader friendly, and evidence based. All of the principles that you have learned and practiced support you in producing an effective executive summary: give your reader easy access to purpose, key points, and evidence in solving the need that you have a passion for addressing. Ask yourself:

- *What is the purpose of my proposal?*
- *What is my unique solution to a critical problem?*
- *Which sections of my document are most important?*
- *What recommendations or course of action do I suggest?*
- *What are the benefits or consequences?*

Application 10.1

Writing a Proposal, Part 1

Instructions: You work for an agency, and your supervisor has asked you and two or three of your co-workers to form a task group. The purpose of your task group will be to identify needs in your community and then write a proposal that will be submitted to a funding foundation.

Your proposal should be between 3 to 5 pages long and include the following:

- Purpose statement, goals, and objectives
- Instruments your task group would use to gather data (such as surveys or assessments)
- Expected outcomes or results
- Strategy for implementing your proposal and time line
- How your agency or task group differentiates itself from others
- Your credentials

Once the proposal is written, you and your group will have an opportunity to give a 5-minute PowerPoint presentation. (See more details in Chapter 12, "Create Engaging Presentations," Application 12.1, page 193.)

For **Part 2** of this project, see Activities 1 – 5, pages 178 – 181 in Chapter 11, "Develop a Task-Group Charter." Chapter 11 provides structure for you and your group in completing this assignment.

Application 10.2

Writing an Executive Summary

Instructions: After you have completed your proposal, write an executive summary. Keep the length of your executive summary to 5 to 10 percent of your entire proposal.

Writers sometimes make the mistake of thinking that they can write an executive summary first and then write the document. This approach results in lost time and frustration. Once you have the evidence, your argument, and your plan, you are far better prepared to write a concise, persuasive executive summary.

Application 10.3

Identifying Resources for Grant Proposal Writing

Instructions: Compile a list of resources that you can use to aid you in writing the various documents related to grants and proposals, such as a letter of inquiry, a cover letter, an executive summary, and even a grant proposal.

For example, one resource, the Foundation Center, http://foundationcenter.org, provides examples of grants that have been funded.

What other resources can you find?

Grant Proposal and Presentation
Scoring Rubric

Criteria	1st Draft Feedback	Final Draft	Points
Appearance			
Cover Letter			
Executive Summary			
Statement of Need			
Program Description / Proposed Services			
Program Goals and Objectives			
Evaluation Plan			
Budget Information			
Letters of Support (3)			
References, if applicable			
Miscellaneous			
Social Work Core Competency 4 Engage in Research-Informed Practice			
Practice Behavior: Translate research evidence to inform and improve practice, policy, service.			
Competency 2 Engage Diversity and Difference in Practice			
Practice Behavior: Apply and communicate understanding of the importance of diversity and difference in shaping life experiences in practice at the micro, mezzo, and macro levels.			
Totals			

(Final 2015 Educational Policy, 2015, http://www.cswe.org/File.aspx?id=79793.)

Informal Proposals

Sharing important ideas in writing rather than verbally improves their prospect of being adopted. At times, you may even turn your idea into a project by presenting it as an informal proposal or **feasibility report or memo**.

Because you build friendly relationships with co-workers, you may not consider turning your ideas into informal proposals. However, your team and supervisors will give your ideas more credence when you put them in writing. A feasibility memo can suggest ways to solve a problem as well as suggest ideas for change: developing a new process or procedure, buying a new product, or revising plans already in progress.

A feasibility report is an abbreviated form of proposal, containing the following basic parts:

1. Briefly discuss the need and your ideas (the proposed project).
2. Outline the benefits of some possible solutions.
3. Give some evaluation criteria.
4. Recommend a solution.

By writing about your ideas, you gain insight into how to present them to others effectively. More importantly, you are able to identify and address some of your readers' questions before they even ask them; hence this approach removes some of the "devil's advocate" type of challenges.

If you give members of your task group a copy of your memo before a meeting, you can incorporate subtle changes and eliminate some concerns *before* your group discusses the merits of your proposed project.

So remember, if you want others to apply your ideas, consider putting them in writing. No one may officially recognize your memo as a feasibility report. However, your memo improves the likelihood of the group adopting your ideas or turning them into projects.

To find out more about feasibility reports, do an Internet search; you can even find templates to use for formal feasibility studies and reports.

References

Shaheen Ashraf-Ahmed, Grant Coordinator, Family Shelter Service, Naperville,

Illinois, authored the cover letter and grant proposal that appear in this chapter.

A. Susan Clarke, MA, MA, LPC, Assistant Director for Research Development, Office of

Research Services, Loyola University Chicago, contributed to this chapter.

The Foundation Center, Proposal Writing Short Course, accessed June 2015

http://foundationcenter.org/getstarted/tutorials/shortcourse/prop1_printNotes

Notes

11

Develop a Task-Group Charter

Effective task-group work and inter-professional collaboration can lead to effective solutions to problems. As well, tapping into various perspectives can strengthen any grant proposal. Before exploring how writing can influence a group's effectiveness, let's review how easy it is for a group to become dysfunctional. Some pitfalls that can affect a group's effectiveness include:

- Going along to get along: *groupthink*
- Becoming too task oriented too soon
- Letting personal friendships and cliques influence decisions
- Discriminating against and blaming group members (consciously or unconsciously)
- Saying one thing in a meeting and another outside of it
- Being controlling rather than sharing the power

Here are some dysfunctional behaviors that can actually tip group dynamics into the toxic range:

- Undervaluing and interrupting
- Sabotaging
- Shaming and blaming
- One-upping
- Being unwilling to share
- Being disengaged and irresponsible
- Being cynical, negative, and self-involved
- Controlling and bullying
- Gossiping
- *Add some of your own . . .*

At first glance, a successful group might seem to be one in which everyone thinks alike, agrees easily, and makes effortless decisions. However, groups function most effectively when members share their perspectives and insights, which can lead to disagreements. Working through these various perspectives can create a very effective project.

Exploring Group Dynamics

The freedom to disagree openly and respectfully is an important quality of successful groups. By developing a level of trust, honesty, and respect, groups are able to have effective discussions that lead to creative, innovative solutions.

To some extent, teamwork is an extension of cultural mores. Some cultures value groups more than others. For example, the Japanese culture is known for effective teamwork, and Japanese communities are known for collaboration. In comparison with people from other cultures, Americans tend to be more independent and competitive, immersed in a culture full of diversity and without cultural traditions that support effective teamwork.

Generally, for Americans to work on a team or in a group without first clearly defining their plan and strategy may lead to challenges. By first defining what they expect to achieve, how they will achieve it, and how they will resolve conflict, teams have a better understanding of their purpose and their individual roles in achieving it.

However, social workers regularly engage in effective teamwork, building communities through collaboration. Social workers participate in staff meetings, treatment team meetings, planning meetings, and advocacy groups, often providing leadership. Each task group must have a leadership team; different group members may be responsible for various tasks, but one or two people must coordinate the work. An effective leader uses social work engagement, listening, planning, and problem-solving skills to facilitate and coordinate the tasks. An agenda, with team-member input, can help organize the meeting and keep the group on task (Fernandez, 1997).

Fernandez (1997) identified five skills to enhance task groups: control, conflict, communication, cohesion, and consensus. First, developing a working relationship and communication among the members is essential. When conflict occurs (*and it will*), respectful communication and relationships are the keys to working through the conflict. Listening to various perspectives, working through misunderstandings, and negotiating can lead to effective outcomes. When group members feel their ideas are heard, supported, and respected, they can become invested in the outcomes and the group forms cohesion (Fernandez, 1997). When group members feel valued, they are more accepting at those times when the group does not follow their solutions or approaches.

Finally, the task group must decide what to do, how to proceed. Consensus is a goal, but sometimes group members have to compromise to reach a decision. For example, three members of your grant-writing task group want to write a grant for an afterschool program *and* a weekend program. However, three other group members think that is taking on too much, and they want to start with an afterschool program. Both programs are needed, but some of the group members are concerned that both programs will stretch the resources and the staff, which could lead to both programs failing. Since all members can agree to support the afterschool program, the group works on this goal.

Though an infinite of ways exist to keep a group from completing its task, only a few clear paths lead to a synchronicity that produces outstanding results. Developing a *group charter* or *agreement* can lead to a common understanding that keeps members focused on their mission.

This chapter gives professionals a "template" for how they can use writing in a group to *get on the same page*, enhancing their ability to achieve their mission.

Forming a Group

First, get to know each other. Find common interests and connections. Exchange contact information and schedules and establish boundaries. For example, some group members who are parents may not want to be called between the hours of 6 and 9 p.m. so that they can spend time with their children.

Before immediately focusing on the work, learn who is interested in what aspect of the task. Figure out a good fit for general tasks. Who might have the time to take on some leadership responsibilities? Identify the researchers, the writers, and the editors. Who will be the time-keeper or take notes this week? Identify the cheer-leaders and supporters who will provide energy and treats during the hard work. One person may take on more than one role.

Answering Core Questions

Core questions relate to a group's **purpose**, **plan**, and **results**. By answering core questions, a group develops an identity that gives it a sense of purpose, building cohesion. In the process, the group also develops criteria on which to judge the merit of ideas and thus avoids some personality clashes or challenges. The focus then becomes analyzing how ideas fit into the mission rather than simply arguing a stance; rather than thwarting diverse views, differences can instead be explored, opening the range of possibilities that may lead to real solutions.

Of course, by answering the core questions below, a group would first need to be fully aware of how its purpose fits into the broader mission of the agency or organization(s) to which the task-group is affiliated. An inter-professional task group may be affiliated with several agencies or organizations.

- What is the group's purpose?
- What are the group's processes? How are decisions made?
- What level of participation is expected from each member?
- How does the group give feedback?
- Do group members understand and respect diversity?

Participation may differ among the members – people do what they can. Let us take a look at each of the above questions, starting with *purpose*.

Purpose   Too often groups assume their purpose is obvious, so they do not "waste" the time to develop a *purpose statement*—or their mission and vision statements, if that applies.

Instead, they become task oriented too quickly. In fact, focusing on tasks at the expense of defining the group can create problems later.

For groups large and small, purpose statements (or *mission* and *vision statements*, if they apply) provide a focus that translates to power, revealing the difference between *what is important* and *what is not*. When groups use these statements to guide their decision-making process, the group's goals, objectives, and action plans have a cohesive baseline to achieve desired results. Only by asking open-ended and hard questions does a group develop a cohesive, powerful core.

In fact, until a group has a *clear and unified sense of purpose*, its efforts will be scattered and disagreement will lead to conflict rather than analysis. Only when everyone shares ownership of goals and objectives as well as their importance do groups have the best chance of functioning effectively.

And make no mistake: writing is the *clarifier* and the *unifier*. Until ideas become words on paper, different members may have various interpretations. By putting points in writing, you ensure that team members have a common understanding of terms and communications. In the example of the task group writing a grant proposal to fund an afterschool program, group members must be clear about the ages of the student participants, the hours, the activities, and location(s) of the program.

Only when information is actually written out and shared can there be the possibility of everyone agreeing about the *same thing*. In other words, without clarifying ideas through the writing process, the idea that one person in the room agrees to may be a different idea from everyone else's. Writing clears out the clutter, forces the fine details, and documents the events.

Processes   So that group members have clear expectations and boundaries, establish leadership, decision-making strategies, and ground rules early on.

By discussing group dynamics openly, members are able to focus on the tasks before group dynamics suffer. For example, *ground rules* help members understand their boundaries and stay on task. When groups write informal *recaps* or formal *minutes* to their meetings, they can establish major decisions as benchmarks.

Recaps help ensure that groups move consistently toward their goals rather than backtrack to rehash controversial issues. Sending an electronic recap (e-recap) prior to the next meeting is a great way to click the "refresh button," getting everyone's focus back on the group's tasks.

Participation   By clearly understanding expectations, members openly become accountable for their share and quality of work. Accountability translates to a sense of fairness. If group members feel they can share their struggles and commitments, more work can be done. For example, Janice says the will miss the next meeting because she has an appointment, so she will take minutes and send them out this week, demonstrating her commitment to the group.

Feedback   By discussing the difference between constructive feedback and criticism, or even negativity, a group encourages accountability and respect. When members receive constructive feedback, less slacking occurs (also known as *freeloading* or *social loafing*). Members are more likely to become active and engaged—or leave the group (either of which is better than carrying *dead weight*).

By aiming feedback at ideas and processes, not individuals, a group may avert personal attacks. Backbiting, bullying, and blaming are destructive and deflate a group's integrity.

Diversity   Functional groups respect diversity, understanding the complexities of personal, ethnic, and generational styles.

For example, when diversity is not respected, extroverted, outgoing group members can easily stifle the quieter, introverted members, limiting creativity and innovation. When generational differences are not understood, diverse styles can easily lead to personal conflict. In contrast, when groups embrace differences in thinking, approaches, and style, disagreement can lead to deeper understanding and more effective outcomes.

When group members are open and honest during a meeting, they frame issues the same regardless of with whom, when, and where they are speaking. An indication that a group is functional and thus effective is when *group members have the same conversation in the meeting as they do in the hallway after they leave.* In other words, the story does not change when the setting changes. In fact, that consistency is also a critical measure of a group's integrity.

One dynamic that can interfere with a group's effectiveness is *groupthink.*

Averting Groupthink

When relationships are more important than mission, a natural result can be *groupthink*. Groupthink does not just inhibit creativity—by definition, groupthink prohibits innovative, creative solutions.

One example is when group members are intimidated by the group leader, perhaps a supervisor. They do not want ask questions to challenge the thinking of the leadership. Therefore, an effective solution or approach may be overlooked. If a supervisor who is responsible for teen activities is put in charge of developing the plan and grant for the afterschool program, her or his approach to youth activities may become the only approach used. If the supervisor is concerned that the teens' grade-point-average is below a "C," then she may focus on tutoring activities in the after-school program. The social activities and snacks may be omitted from the plan. However, if group members feel comfortable to contribute, and their suggestions are welcomed, then they may suggest additional activities. They may suggest that first some snacks and social activities would draw the teens into the program. Later, they could settle down for some tutoring, followed by more social activities as a reward.

When team members make their relationships primary to their mission, fear and insecurity can drive group dynamics, especially for those members "left out in the cold."

Groups can avert groupthink, in part, by developing a group charter. In the process of developing a group charter, they also put the mission front and center, developing an effective strategy for success.

Writing a Task-Group Charter

Task groups or teams can easily fall into the trap of being too task oriented too soon, succumbing to the anxiety of impending deadlines. However, without a plan, group members may not be working on the *right* tasks. This section walks you through the questions that lead to a charter (see page 182 for a *template* to develop your task group or team charter).

Rather than letting a deadline lead the process, instead start the planning process by establishing a common understanding—*getting everyone on the same page*, so to speak. By establishing purpose and plan up front, a group will have sufficient time to achieve their goals.

To develop cohesion, first define *what* your group will do and then *how* the group will do it. Use questions to reach that common understanding: reframe the basic six questions—*who, what, when, where, why,* and *how*—to establish goals that lead to objectives and an action plan.

Goals tend to control objectives; for example:

- A **goal** is a long-term intention of what your group will achieve; goals are general and are not necessarily measureable.
- An **objective** is a smaller step: a specific result of what your group will achieve within a defined time frame. Use the acronym **SMART** when you develop objectives:

> **S**pecific
> **M**easureable
> **A**chievable
> **R**elevant
> **T**imely

If it applies, also be clear about **audience**:

- Who will decide if the plan will be approved or the grant will be funded?
- Who are the stakeholders, the supporters that want to see the services implemented?
- What are their needs and expectations?
- What is their measure of success?

Regardless of how the group collects the details, putting them on paper is important. Recording preliminary discussions through a map or chart establishes progress and aids those whose primary learning style is visual.

Developing Purpose, Plan, and Results

Defining your *purpose, plan,* and *results* develops a framework for any type of group project.

Defining Purpose   *Purpose* embodies the *what* and *why* of the problem: a *purpose statement* defines your project.

1. *What is your **purpose statement**?* Start by asking, *what is the critical problem that your group is solving?* Then, state the problem and your solution in one sentence.

For example, if the youth you are serving are getting in trouble after school before their parents return home and your job is to help them solve the problem, your purpose statement might read:

Develop a plan to create and fund an afterschool program.

Develop two or three statements before selecting the best one as your working purpose statement. From a purpose statement, a group can develop goals and objectives, clarify the methods they will use to solve the problem, and even identify the results they will achieve. As you work through the process, the purpose statement may be modified as the project develops.

2. *What are your* **project goals**? *What are three to five goals that support your purpose statement?*

   Drawing from the example about an afterschool program for teens, here are some goals:

   • Identify root causes for the youth getting in trouble.
   • Develop and fund a program that addresses the root causes.
   • Implement the program.
   • Measure the delinquent activity after school before and after the program is implemented.

Once again, *goals* are broad and somewhat abstract, *objectives* are specific and measureable. By first defining goals, you can then develop specific objectives to provide the roadmap to achieving your purpose.

3. *What are the group's* **objectives**? After defining goals, identify individual objectives and tasks or action steps. Continuing with the example about employee attendance, here are some objectives relating to the first goal:

   o   To identify root causes of our neighborhood youth engaging in delinquent behavior after school, we need to conduct focus groups, talk to police, and/or conduct individual interviews with the youth and their parents.
   o   To conduct focus groups, we need to develop a list of relevant questions.

Based on objectives, tasks will unfold as the group develops *flow* with the project, which you can add to an ongoing *task log*. Use charts with *post-it* notes or a white board. Or use an electronic method such as, *Google.docs* or *GoToMeeting*, which allows several people to modify a document at the same time. Devise your own creative way to keep track of ideas.

Forming an Action Plan:
Tasks, Action Steps, and Time Frame

An *action plan* anchors group activities by identifying tangible milestones to measure progress.

What are the specific tasks or action steps? Once you identify tasks, turn them into *action steps* by determining who will complete the task and by what date. The tasks need to be measurable, specific, and attainable.

Continuing with the example of the afterschool program, here are some action steps:

1. Develop focus group questions. (Marcie and Alice; due: May 15)
2. Hold three focus groups, one for young men (Joe, June 5), one for young women (Alice, June 7), and one for parents (Marcie June 1).
3. Analyze the results. (Joe, Alice, and Marcie; due: June 30)

Your task log will change as your project develops; be flexible in the way that you accomplish your goals. Embrace your group members' unique styles and ways of thinking: use diversity to enrich your project, not side-track it.

Planning Logistics or Group Operations

Early in the project, identify methods to achieve your objectives by connecting the questions *who, when, where,* and *how* to group operations (logistics), the tasks, and the time frame.

1. *How will we conduct task meetings?*
   o Who should we include in the grant-writing team—a parent and a teen, the principal, a police officer?
   o Where will we meet and when? How often?
   o How will we establish decisions (consensus, majority rules)?
   o What are our ground rules?
   o Will we prepare agendas?
   o Will we keep minutes?
   o How will we keep each other informed (especially when someone misses a meeting)?

2. *What is the time line?*

   o What is the deadline? For example, when is the grant due? Do we want to start the afterschool program by next fall?

   o What are some milestones or internal deadlines?

   o How often will we meet and where?

   o What are some milestones or internal deadlines?

   o How often will we meet and where?

   o How will holidays and other events affect our schedule?

3. *What tools or resources do we need to accomplish our tasks?*

   o Do we need laptops, white boards, flip charts, or mapping software?

   o Do we need to develop surveys?

   o Do we need to conduct interviews?

   o Where will our resources come from?

4. *How will we know if we are accomplishing our objectives?*

   o How will we give each other feedback?

   o What happens if someone does not fulfill his or her role?

   o What degree of flexibility will we tolerate when someone misses meetings or deadlines?

What questions does your group need to answer?

Determining Results   *What are the expected outcomes?*

   o What programs will we develop or change?

   o What new policies will we implement?

   o What new skills will employees develop?

   o How will our outcomes help people, improve systems, or change programs?

You could take the extra step to relate your results to your agency's vision or mission. By doing this, you are placing your project in a context, thereby highlighting its importance in broader understanding of community service provision. Also, if your research uncovers next steps or leads to new topics to examine, include these in your results.

One final question you may want to ask: *What do group members expect to gain personally from participating?* The more invested group members are in achieving outcomes, the more driven they will be to achieve group objectives. Groups can nurture individual interests by discussing how members can personally benefit by achieving group goals. These might include promotions, resolving a problem that is impacting her or him, or reducing a social problem.

Identifying Roles

If a group chooses to assign roles, the most basic roles are *facilitator* and *record keeper*. However, these roles do not need to be static but can change for every meeting. In fact, once a group defines its goals, all members can define clear roles in achieving the group's objectives.

- A **facilitator** leads the group discussion, creating an agenda if feasible. Some groups have co-facilitators, one to focus on the group process while the other focuses on content. The facilitator(s) can take an active role by collecting ideas on a flip chart or white board; the facilitator directs the discussion by encouraging one speaker at a time. The facilitator also determines when the group is ready to make a decision or move on to a new topic. Effective facilitators often withhold their opinions and judgments and use open-ended questions to solicit responses. "What if" questions encourage the task group to expand on ideas and think through the consequences of various approaches and decisions.

- A **record keeper** records decisions and other details, such as information generated on a flip chart or white board. A record keeper may use a cellphone to record a meeting and would provide a recap or minutes of meetings, presenting them at the beginning of the next meeting or prior to it.

If the group wants to delineate roles further, it can appoint a *timekeeper* who would subtly inform the facilitator when time has expired on a topic and the group needs to move on. Another role that could be filled is that of *devil's advocate*, a role that would provide reasons why some of the group's choices might not work as planned. This role helps the group avoid group think.

Always remain aware that special relationships with group members create a situation that is ripe for conflict. Close alliances can cause friction and develop a *split* in the group (that is, even small issues can become controversial, with group members dividing and taking sides). In group activities, treat friends impartially; this boundary helps you maintain trust with other members.

The group can evaluate the meeting by doing a summary or a *plus-delta feedback* process at the end of the meeting (which will take perhaps 5 minutes). The goal of the plus-delta feedback activity is to help the group function more effectively, even though the group may not be able to make all of the changes suggested. Members should be realistic about limitations.

Plus-Delta Feedback

To organize feedback, the evaluator could facilitate a plus-delta activity. The *plus* stands for what worked and *delta* stands for what should be changed. On a flip chart or white board, put a plus sign (+) at the top of one column and a delta sign (Δ) at the top of a second column. First fill in the plus column and then seek to keep balance by putting items in the delta column.

For example:

+	Δ
The agenda was clear.	*We spent too much time off topic and should have become focused sooner.*

Establishing Ground Rules

During your first or second meeting, take the time to establish *working agreements*, and then periodically revisit them. If you prefer, use the term *guidelines* or *best practices*.

Here is a starting point for defining ground rules:

1. Everyone will be open and honest.

2. Everyone will have a say and be heard.

3. Everyone will listen respectfully to each other without argument or negative reaction, remaining open and positive.

When conflict occurs, revisit your purpose and ground rules, seeking agreement among group members to do the following:

- Ask questions to draw out various aspects of the conflict.

- Support opinions by data or examples of specific behavior.

- Listen without judging.

- Avoid interrupting, blaming, and arguing.

- Ask for feedback to check understanding.

- Ask for a commitment to working out a solution.

- Check to see if the group needs training on topics such as diversity, communication, or conflict resolution.

- Set goals, create an action plan, and follow up on your solution.

Giving Feedback

To keep communication flowing, group members must periodically give each other feedback. Here are some guidelines.

1. *Describe behavior rather than evaluate it.*

   Describing relates to giving specific details as to what happened; *evaluating* relates to judging (or criticizing) the behavior. To avoid evaluating, focus on what happened without interpreting the behavior or implying how it affected group dynamics.

   Evaluating: George disrupted the meeting and created problems when he was late.

   Describing: George was 10 minutes late for the meeting.

2. *Be specific rather than general.*

   A general comment does not provide the listener with concrete information, so often the main point remains misunderstood.

   General: You don't treat people with respect.

   Specific: You seemed to interrupt Sue several times during the meeting.

3. *Use I statements.*

When giving verbal feedback on challenging issues, shape your words so that you do not sound accusatory. By using an *I statement*, you can keep the focus on how the behavior affected you.

Here is a three-part approach for *I statements*:

1. How do you feel?   *I feel frustrated*

2. Why?   *when I do not receive reports on time*

3. Because?   *because I cannot meet my deadlines.*

Here's another example:

You statement: You are accusing me for the entire problem.

I statement: When I heard that comment, I felt devastated because I felt that I was being accused for the entire problem.

Your goal is to keep attention on the *behavior* and *your feelings*—not the other person. By taking ownership of your feelings and speaking about your own feelings, you are more likely to ensure that the other person listens to what you are saying. In addition, people can argue about what seem to be accusations against them, but they cannot legitimately argue with you about your feelings or thoughts.

When a serious issue exists, meet in person and in private. If you need to document concerns, wait until after you have spoken: you may clarify misunderstandings as you discuss the issues together.

4. *Use the Passive Voice, the Tactful Voice.*

When you communicate about sensitive issues, consider using the passive voice. With the passive voice, you can leave people out of the statement and focus on the issue, which allows those involved to take responsibility or make amends without feeling unduly targeted.

Active: You were wrong not to bring the information to the group.

Passive: The information should have been brought   to the group.

The passive voice is perfect for situations that have the potential to involve blame:

Active: You made a mistake on the research.

Passive: A mistake was made on the research.

Active: You did not inform George about the change.

Passive: George was not informed about the change.

When speaking about a problem, the tone sounds less accusatory by not pointing a finger. Not holding someone accountable is an important quality at times.

If you use the passive voice when you give constructive feedback, the listener is more likely hear the message. You can add an *I statement* to further cushion the information.

For example: I feel that the decision should have been brought to the entire group. I hope that next time we will have the opportunity to decide.

5. *Turn Negative Feedback into Constructive Feedback.*

The goal of feedback is to change behavior, not to hurt the person receiving it. When you give feedback, be constructive rather than negative.

- **Negative feedback** identifies the problem but not the solution.

- **Constructive feedback** identifies the problem, offers a possible solution, and opens a dialog.

Constructive feedback is not accusatory; it gets the involved persons talking. However, when feedback is conveyed ineffectively, the person receiving it can feel attacked.

Give PCS Feedback: Positive – Constructive – Supportive

1. Start with an honest, *positive* statement,

2. State the *constructive* feedback, and finally,

3. End on a *supportive* note.

Here is an example of constructive feedback following a Positive – Constructive – Supportive pattern:

George, you are always so motivated when a project begins, and your motivation adds energy to the project. However, I've noticed that the project is behind schedule because your piece has not yet been completed. Is there anything I can do to assist you?

Constructive Feedback and Requests

With communication, recipes usually do not work well. That is because communication must remain interactive; at its best, communication is an interchange, an honest exchange between human beings.

However, since giving constructive feedback or making a request can be difficult, here is a pattern to use to keep the discussion focused when addressing something that affects you personally.

First, state the problem and how it affects you; for example:

When you give me reports late (or: When I receive reports late),*

I cannot complete my work on time, and as a result I feel as if my time is not being respected.

Next, state what the person can do to solve the problem; for example:

My request is that you get me the work on time; and if you cannot make the deadline, let me know in advance.

Finally, open a dialog by asking if the person could change the behavior; for example:

Could you do that for me?

Now, think of a current situation and fill in the blanks below.

When (you)*_____, I feel_____. Therefore, I would appreciate it if you would_____.

Would you be willing to_____?

*When you can, state the problem using the *I viewpoint*.

It takes courage to give and receive constructive feedback, but it can change ineffective behavior and help improve relationships.

The best time to address inappropriate behavior is soon after the behavior occurs. However, also give constructive feedback when neither the speaker nor the listener feels emotional about it. When you can, wait until things settle down.

The way that feedback is given (and received) can enhance or damage a relationship. If you have doubts about how to convey feedback, role-play the situation or talk with your supervisor.

6. *Avoid Trigger Words.*

Some other words that trigger a negative emotional response are *unsatisfactory, unacceptable, unfair, not, never . . . had enough? Never again . . . .* These can seem like *micro-aggressions* to the recipient, especially to a group member who has less power than you, such as a teen, parent, or advocate.

Do Not Say: This research is unacceptable and will not support the project.

Do Say: As soon as you are able to find more sources that fit what is needed, we will be able to move forward to the next phase of the project.

7. *Beware of micro-messages: written, spoken, and nonverbal.*

Group members are sensitive to micro-messages: the real message that occurs *between the lines.*

Especially in meetings, be aware of your nonverbal signals. When members roll their eyes, shrug their shoulders, or shake their heads in disapproval, a dynamic may be set in motion that creates hidden conflict. Even tightly folded arms during a heated discussion can give the impression that the listener is closed or angry. Keep your body relaxed and remain aware that your gestures make a difference.

Receiving Feedback

How you receive feedback is also important. When receiving feedback, focus on the content, not on the person.

1. Assume the person giving the feedback is concerned about the work, not personal differences.

2. Focus on the three most common reasons for constructive feedback: to improve skills, quality, or outcomes.

3. Listen calmly and attentively to the whole statement to get the complete picture.

4. Tune in fully: your willingness to listen may make the speaker feel better by showing that you are engaged.

5. Monitor any negative reactions you have to keep them from escalating

6. Refrain from disagreeing or arguing.

7. Clarify the feedback by asking *a few questions* to understand the situation fully; however, asking a lot of questions may aggravate the situation.

8. Acknowledge the other person's concerns, showing that you understand the other person's point of view.

9. Before responding in detail, ask if you can have some time to reflect upon what you have just learned.

10. Point to common goals and objectives.

11. Thank the person for taking the time to discuss the issue with you.

12. Express your willingness to engage in mutual problem solving.

13. Reflect on the experience and put it in perspective

14. Get a good night's rest before you make important decisions.

Tapping into each other's strengths and then working in constructive ways to complete the task leads to an effective group process. Listen with an open mind until you can work through to a win-win solution.

Writing in a Group

From rough draft to final copy, you can do group writing projects in various ways. Here are a few suggestions:

1. *Map out the various parts or sections.* Start with a *concept map* (which is similar to a *mind map*). The group may start with an outline, if one is provided. Identifying each major component of the project, creating a visual so that you can see how the pieces fit together. With certain types of documents, such as proposals, standard parts can be identified immediately. (Also note that free mapping software is available online: simply do a search on "free mind mapping software.")

2. *Research and become familiar with the content and topics.* Fill in details as you go along, using post-it notes or any other creative tool you can devise.

3. *Brainstorm ideas together.* Assign a facilitator to lead brain-storming sessions at any phase. (If feasible, use a laptop, flip chart, or white board).

4. *Coordinate writing assignments with task assignments.* In this way, group members and partners write about tasks they complete and about familiar topics.

5. *Map pages and compose together or alone.* Mind map each part and turn mind maps into *page maps*. Then compare notes.

6. *Respect differences in learning styles and personality styles.* Some members work better alone than they do in a group; a group can respect that style through individual tasks rather than forced partnerships.

7. *Establish reasonable due dates.* Group members need to have clear expectations; allow room for error because unforeseen circumstances can arise—that means setting *internal due dates* in ample time to meet *external due dates.*

8. *Evaluate and revise your draft together:*

    o   Agree up front that every draft will need at least one revision.

    o   Allow time for silent reading *before* discussing a section.

    o   Give suggestions for improving the document rather than criticizing it.

9. *Bring the parts together for a final editing.* Write your project in a consistent voice; early on, identify the member who is the most competent writer/editor and reserve that individual's time for the final edit.

10. *Recognize each other for effort that results in work well done!*

Finally, ask for help when you need it. When life happens, let other group members know so that you can avoid surprises that result in frustration for your group.

Workshop Assignments

Application 11.1

Writing a Proposal, Part 2

Instructions: Once you know the members of your task group, you are *almost* ready to start developing the details of your proposal.

One mistake that groups make is to start finding answers before they agree on the questions. Another is to shortchange themselves by not getting to know their team members along with their strengths and weaknesses.

Thus, you may want to spend the first project meeting establishing how your group will make decisions, establishing ground rules, scheduling meetings, and developing a time line . . . *as well as getting to know one another.*

Application 11.2

Task Group Meeting

Instructions: Since task groups accomplish projects through a series of meetings, your first goal is to get to know each other and get focused on your project. Attend your first group meeting, and as a group see which of the following you can accomplish:

1. Do a warm-up activity or check in. (See Activity 11.3)
2. Identify how your group will facilitate meetings and make decisions; for example, *will you appoint a facilitator, recorder, and evaluator?*
3. Develop ground rules. (See Activity 11.4)
4. Identify topics for your proposal or group project.
5. Compose a rough purpose statement (which can be revised at the next meeting).
6. Develop a timeline and a meeting schedule.
7. Assign tasks. *What preparation should each member make for the next meeting?*
8. What products will the group generate to meet the project's requirement?

By the end of the first meeting, a task group has accomplished a great deal if they leave feeling as if they are "all on the same page." *Has your group developed a common understanding of the project? Which of the above items do you need to carry over into your next meeting? Will someone prepare an agenda for the next meeting?*

Application 11.3

Warm-Up Activities or Check In

Instructions: Beyond simple introductions, you may want to use a warm-up activity (or *check in*) so that you and your group members can learn more about each other's background and interests. A warm-up activity gets group members focused on the meeting and builds respect and trust, qualities which contribute to a group's success.

Here is a sampling of questions that you can use:

1. Give three words to describe your mood or what you are feeling about the project.

2. What's up with you right now?

3. What is something people would not know about you just by looking at you?

Now, develop a question or two of your own.

1.

2.

Identify a maximum amount of time your group will spend on these activities; for example, tell each member they have about 1 minute to speak. You may be surprised to learn that some group members will speak for only a few seconds and others, well . . . *staying within boundaries helps everyone!*

Application 11.4

Developing Ground Rules

Instructions: Just as successful meetings depend on shared expectations, so do group activities. Thus, successful groups often establish ground rules so members share expectations through established boundaries.

Here is a sampling of some ground rules:

1. People are free to express feelings as well as ideas.

2. Members agree to give feedback relating to ideas rather than personal criticism.

3. Members agree to follow through on their agreements or inform the group when they are not able to meet their obligations.

4. Members agree to keep controversial issues open for discussion.

5. Members agree to keep what's spoken in the room among the members, unless consultation is needed.

6. Members give the facilitator permission to manage the meeting process.

When your group meets to adopt its own ground rules, you can refer to this list. However, by creating your own list (even if the ideas are similar), your group will take ownership of them.

What are your group's ground rules? Before adopting them, your group facilitator should ask if anyone has anything to change or add. When finalizing the ground rules, silence does not mean agreement; ask that each member either give a nod or raise a hand to show agreement.

Application 11.5

Understanding How Groups Function

Background: In 1965, Bruce W. Tuckman wrote an article entitled "Developmental Sequence in Small Groups" (Psychological Bulletin, No. 63, 1965, pp. 384-399). In the article, Tuckman outlined stages of group development, and his model has become a classic in the field.

In 2014, Seck and Helton described an update and utilization of Tuckman's approach by social work faculty in Faculty Development of a Joint MSW Program Utilizing Tuckman's Model of Stages of Group Development. *Social Work with Groups, 37*(2), 158-168.

Instructions: Research Tuckman's theory as well as social work perspectives on how groups function. Then write your professor a process message describing some of the approaches you learned as well as sharing some of your own group experiences.

- How does your experience or practice relate to theory?

- Have you ever been in a group that could have been more functional? If so, what are some ways the group could have improved its process?

Application 11.6

Analyzing Team Dynamics

Instructions: At a team meeting, play the role of evaluator. At the end of the meeting, facilitate a plus-delta activity. After the meeting, compare your perceptions with your teammates' perceptions.

- Who was the natural leader?
- Who was a note taker?
- Who sat back and said/did nothing?
- Do you agree or disagree with the group's assessment?
- Do you have other points to add?

Write a process message to your instructor summarizing the group's feedback followed by your insights.

Template for Task-Group Charter

Task Description

Purpose | Duration | Timeline

Members

Purpose Statement | Mission Statement

Task-Group Goals

Action Plan (who, what, and when)

      Tasks | Time frame

Workload Distribution

Due Dates

Ground Rules and Guidelines

Resources

Reporting Plan

Outcomes | Results

To print out a detailed template:

1. Go to **www.thewriterstoolkit.com**
2. Click on the **Templates** tab.
3. Finally, click on **Team Charter** for the template.

Notes

12

Create Engaging
Presentations

PowerPoint—along with Prezi and other presentation tools—has the potential to be overused and misused, which is how the phrase "death by PowerPoint" became popular. Especially when information is complicated, presenters need to adapt to the needs of their audience.

By understanding the purpose of PowerPoint (and other options, such as Prezi), presenters can use options to provide complicated information in an engaging way. Though this may take more work in planning and preparation, audiences deserve that respect. Wasting someone's time creates stress. Doing the work up front is what it takes to achieve outstanding results.

For ease of discussion, reference is made to PowerPoint throughout this chapter; however, the theory for developing a PowerPoint presentation applies to Prezi and other similar software.

Workshop 12 Inventory

Instructions: Read and answer the questions below.

1. A PowerPoint (PP) presentation should tell "the whole story."   T/F

2. In general, rich designs are preferred over simple designs for PP slides.   T/F

3. Which type of font is recommended for PP slides:

   a. serif   b. non-serif

4. Especially complicated information should be presented on slides.   T/F

5. To make slides easier to read, use acronyms and abbreviations.   T/F

6. Limit the amount of text to no more than fifteen words per line.   T/F

7. Put up to 15 lines as long as you reduce your font size.   T/F

Note: See page 236 for the key to this inventory.

Let no one underestimate the fear and anxiety that someone experiences at the idea of presenting in front of a live audience. Most people go to great extremes to avoid being criticized, and that dynamic can lead to procrastination. By avoiding the inevitable, presenters lose the time that they need to learn their topic, simplify it, prepare supporting material, and develop creative ways to engage their audience.

Let's start with purpose and then walk through a process to help you *prepare, practice,* and *present.*

Respect the Purpose

PowerPoint slides are not meant to tell the whole story. That is the presenter's job. PowerPoint slides should also not be used to present complicated information; that is what additional handouts are for.

Every PowerPoint presentation should aim to engage the audience so that they interact with the information; otherwise, the presentation is a one-way communication. People do not learn well when information comes to them in a rapid-fire manner—this approach leads to information overload.

Use PowerPoint slides to present key concepts and ideas. After you identify what you want your audience to remember afterward, use slides to engage them in a learning process about those key ideas.

By the way, professionals are often relieved when they learn that they will attend an event that does *not* involve a PowerPoint. By relying on flip charts and white boards, you are using tools to support interacting with your audience. As a presenter, you would ask for audience input to generate information, writing it on the flip chart. Therefore, even when you present a PowerPoint, incorporate flip charts, sticky notes, or white boards to ensure that your presentation is interactive.

The best use for PowerPoint is for short presentations that include large audiences. Even then, the presenter is the focus, using slides only to highlight key ideas.

When you learn your topic well enough to teach it in a simple way, your audience will walk away with something they can use, feeling satisfied for time well spent.

Everything should be made as simple as possible but not simpler.

—Albert Einstein

Prepare

Prepare your presentation in a systematic manner similar to the way you prepare other forms of communication. Keep in mind that preparing is not a linear, step-by-step process. Working on any part at any time will contribute to the success of the whole.

Here are steps that lead to effective presentations:

1. Determine the purpose
2. Identify the audience
3. Develop your topic: map it out
4. Choose a design for your slides
5. Sketch our your plan
6. Compose with text and graphics
7. Do not overuse animated graphics
8. Format each slide
9. For group presentations, put your initials on slides containing information you provided (to avoid plagiarism issues)
10. Edit text and graphics
11. Add citations on slides, as needed, and include a reference list at the end
12. Prepare your handouts

Remember that some people in the audience may be visually impaired so avoid using graphics such as flipping dinosaurs and flying balloons.

After you prepare meticulously, you will practice and present with ease.

Determine the Purpose
Start with your objectives: what do you want to achieve? Think in terms of your topic and your audience.

In the beginning stages of preparing, all of your attention is on your topic because you are still learning it: learning occurs at various levels. As you teach a concept, you learn it at deeper levels.

Therefore, even if you are knowledgeable in an area, you are facing a learning curve that may feel uncomfortable: it is not your topic that is key—it is presenting the topic so that your audience has a learning experience, not just a listening experience.

What ideas or principles do you want your audience to apply to make their lives or work simpler and more effective?

Identify the Audience   Who is your audience? How many will be part of it? What is their background? What are their *pain points*—what is a topic that will help your audience solve some sort of problem? What do they already know about the topic?

- Regardless of the topic, keep it as simple as possible.

- Define your terms to create a common understanding of the topics

- Avoid abbreviations, acronyms, and initialisms: even within organizations, jargon causes confusion.

- Respect cultural differences by using common words.

- Avoid slang, cultural terms, and idioms, which can cause audience members who do not understand the reference to feel left out.

By discussing your topic with others, you learn about their experiences, questions, and frustrations, further helping you to mold your topic to the needs of an audience.

Develop Your Topic: Map it Out   If needed, start by writing about the topic until you can identify your key points. As discussed in chapter 1, develop a mind map, a page map, or even a traditional outline if you know your topic well enough.

If you are uncomfortable using PowerPoint or another presentation software, consider *storyboarding* to plan your slides. To storyboard, turn your paper horizontally so that its layout is landscape (sideways). Then draw a line down the middle, and put your text on one side of the sheet and a sketch of a graphic on the other. In planning your graphics, consider browsing for clip art.

Your graphics should convey a message, not just entertain. When selecting your graphics, consider the *tone* you wish to convey. For a more professional tone, you might use only photos; whereas for a lighter tone, you might use cartoons. When in doubt, stay conservative. In any case, jot down the image or the file name in your storyboard across from your text.

Choose a Design for your Slides   Part of planning the organization and content of your slides includes choosing a functional and attractive template. An almost infinite number of designs are available free online.

- Choose a simple theme that will complement, not compete with your message.

- Select colors that contrast to enhance ease of reading.

- Use a non-serif font such as Arial or Calibri because their simplicity makes them easier to read from a distance. (Serif fonts such as Times New Roman are still the best choice for print.)

Sketch Your Plan   Transfer the information that you generate from your mind map, outline, or storyboard to slides.

- Decide on your *major headers*, which will each then be titles for individual slides.
- Create one slide for each major header.
- Divide each header into *sub-topics* or *second-level headers*.
- Divide each of your subtopics further, if necessary.

If an outline has been provided for an assignment, use the outline points for some of your headings.

Compose with Text and Graphics   Begin to build each slide with these outcomes in mind:

- As a general rule, limit the amount of your text to no more than *eight words per line* and *no more than eight lines per slide*; some guidelines recommend even fewer.
- Create a short introduction and a brief conclusion. (Write the introduction and conclusion last to make sure they are consistent with your presentation.)
- If needed, include *transitional slides* that introduce new sections or summarize what preceded them.
- For large groups, use fewer words and larger print.
- Use animation sparingly: too much animation can be worse than none at all, especially for those in your audience who are visually impaired or forgot their glasses.

The time you are investing will pay off in a multitude of ways—the repetition you go through as you review each slide prepares you to present with confidence.

Format Each Slide   As you format, add slides as needed so that your audience can read with ease.

- Set the size of the font so that those in the back of the room can read the slides (for example, use at least size 30 font in a large room).
- Break up information and add slides as needed to keep font size readable.
- Include *white space* around your text to improve readability.
- Limit the number of words, the size of your graphics, and the colors you use.
- Keep in mind that light-colored fonts may look fine on your computer screen but can

seem washed out and be difficult to read when projected on a large screen; dark backgrounds make some fonts/colors hard to read.

- Be wary of using too many *effects* or changing them too often. Having your words fly in from the left or having slides change like vertical blinds can work well, but mixing too many effects distracts your audience.

Edit Text and Graphics As you edit, arrange your slides in a logical order, placing transitional slides appropriately.

- Check and cite your data.
- Edit each slide for accuracy, clarity, consistency, and conciseness.
- Cut unnecessary words and graphics: *When in doubt, cut it out--less is more.* Cutting is the painful part of editing, but your results are better.
- Use parallel structure: present your bullet points in the same grammatical form: noun for noun, verb for verb.
- Use active voice when feasible.
- Eliminate excess graphics.

If you are presenting with a group, include the initials of the person or people providing the data on each slide to avoid plagiarism.

Finally, make sure that each slide presents information so that everyone in your room can read it easily, regardless of where they are sitting: when you present, you will discuss the information on each slide, *but you will not read your slides to your audience.* Your goal is to be concise, clear, consistent, and accurate, using your PowerPoint as a guide but not a crutch.

Prepare Your Handouts   Handouts are not only good tools for your audience, they provide a backup for you in case of any sort of system failure. When you print your slides:

- Select the *Handout* option.
- Select the number of slides per page: 3 to 6 slides allows your audience to take notes effectively.
- Select the *Pure Black and White* option for a crisp, clear copy.

When information becomes complicated, prepare it as a separate handout.

Practice

Regardless of whether your audience will consist of 5 people or 100 people, practice rehearsing—speaking your presentation aloud—until you feel confident.

The best way to practice is to record yourself. If you do not have access to video recording, recording only audio works well. (Many phones now have these tools available.) Listening to your own voice as you present your topic is the absolute best way to notice subtleties so that you can fine-tune your words.

Listening to yourself also helps you memorize your presentation, building your confidence. In contrast, if you present to a peer, you may find that you are interrupted at key moments, causing needless frustration. And frustration is the last thing you need. If you need to practice in front of someone, hire a professional coach who knows how and when to give feedback.

On the day of your presentation, ensure that all seating has good visual access to your presentation. If people cannot read your presentation, you will lose their attention. They will leave disappointed, even if you talk them through it.

Present

Reading PowerPoint slides is no more effective than reading a typed speech. As you speak, consider eye contact and voice as well as your interaction with your slides and audience.

- In a room of 20 to 25 people, make eye contact with everyone at least once.
- With a large audience, look around as you speak and try to make contact with as many people as possible.
- Since the audience reads slides from left to right, you create a better flow by standing on the right side of the screen (from your audience's perspective).
- As you present, consider your *voice projection, pronunciation,* and *speed.*
    - Project your voice so that the people in the back of the room can hear it.
    - Practice pronouncing any words that you anticipate having difficulty saying.
    - Modulate your speed—speaking slowly at times and even pausing.
- Point to the slides and comment on individual terms.
- Interact with the audience by asking questions, even if you do not expect answers.
- Do not read your slides or "hide behind them": interact with your slides and audience, referring to your slides and elaborating on parts of each.
- Once again, speak slowly: the faster you speak, the more nervous you may feel.

If you feel confident, include a short activity in which you present the audience with a question; then give them a short time (not more than 5 minutes) to discuss with a partner or small group. However, if you are not confident or prepared enough, you may have difficulty regaining control and the presentation will feel chaotic.

Let It Flow

Prepare meticulously—do not let your fears hold you back. When you make a mistake, let it go quickly. Only you know what you had planned to say or do. Even if you have problems with logistics, stay confident and upbeat. Your audience will take your lead. As a wise mother once said, learn how to *act confident* and you will *feel confident*.

In the end, the only one who will give your mistakes a second thought is you—so do not spend any time after your presentation dwelling on what you should have done. If you make a mistake, appreciate the learning opportunity and move on. The key to doing a great job is preparing well and then going with the flow.

Use *Signal Anxiety* to Your Benefit

Signal anxiety is a healthy type of anxiety that tugs at your sleeve, gently reminding you to start working. However, rather than working on an unimportant task to relieve your feelings, take action on the task that you are avoiding, the one that has the impending deadline. You will feel instant relief and see immediate results.

As you take action, do not try to start from the beginning. Write about what you know first. Let what you already know lead you to fresh insights. In fact, once you start writing, you gain deeper insight, even when you are not thinking about your topic.

Writing forces you to make progress by pulling you to deeper levels of understanding. That is why writing sometimes feels painful: putting critical thoughts on paper takes energy and courage because you force yourself to take positions, make decisions, and think clearly.

Writing is a problem-solving activity: writing is *thinking on paper*.

Trust the process.

Application 12.1

Develop a PowerPoint for Your Proposal

Instructions: The funding agency received a copy of your proposal and would like to know more about it. As a result, you have been invited to the funding agency's offices to do a formal presentation about the details of your proposal.

The funding organization will make their vendor-selection decision after you and several other agencies have presented their proposals. Your PowerPoint should take about 5 minutes to present and "tell the story" of your proposal.

Application 12.2

Analyze Presentation Tools

Instructions: Tamburro (2010) created a Prezi using the medicine wheel framework to explain the interconnection among the various aspects of social work curriculum. Here is the link to Tamburro's Prezi, *Weaving Social Work Education into Effective Practice Using the Medicine Wheel*:

https://prezi.com/wtullka_cptx/weaving-social-work-education-into-effective-practice/

After watching the Prezi, discuss it with a partner or your team.

- How does Prezi compare with PowerPoint?
- What other presentation tools are available?
- Which tool do you prefer and why?
- What are some keys to doing an effective presentation regardless of the tool that you use?

Notes

Best Practices for
E-Communication

The vast majority of professionals have received no training about how to write effective e-mail. Unlike protocol for hard copy correspondence, e-communication continues to mutate and evolve.

Because of these factors, e-mail is not necessarily as easy to manage as professionals sometimes like to think.

E-Mail Inventory

Instructions: Read and answer the questions below.

1. To save time, the best way to manage e-mail is to read "on demand." T/ F

2. When conveying bad news, it is best to get to the point. T/F

3. Some messages have an emotional overtone and should be responded to in the same kind of tone. T/F

4. In general, give an explanation before stating the main point. T/F

5. For urgent messages, e-mail is the best communication option. T/F

6. Respond to all e-mail messages within a day or two, even when you have doubts about your message. T/F

7. E-mail messages are legal documents. T/F

8. An indirect purpose of professional communication is to:

    a. inform   b. persuade   c. build client relationships

9. When you don't want to speak to someone, e-mail is your best option. T/F

10. Have you ever sent an e-mail message that you wish you hadn't sent? Yes/No

Note: See page 236 for the key to this inventory.

Professional Communication

Have you ever been upset because you received an e-mail that sounded accusatory? Or have you ever sent a message that you wish you could have retrieved as soon as you hit the *send* button?

If you find yourself avoiding someone, e-mail should not be your communication mode of choice. Phone the person or walk over to his or her office and have a brief chat. Seeing someone's face or hearing that person's voice can magically melt tension in a way that e-mail cannot. In fact, e-mail has a tendency to perpetuate problems, if not escalate them.

When you feel hurt or reach a point of exhaustion leading you to think that you do not care about outcomes, walk away from the computer. When making your point is more important than how it will affect others, either stop for the day or take a break. If you need to respond right away, acknowledge the message and let the person know that you need more time.

An underlying purpose of all professional communication is to build relationships, and that includes e-mail. If you start down a negative e-mail conversation with a colleague, assert a more positive attitude and work to dissolve the issue. Otherwise, you may find yourself losing energy and credibility with your colleagues. You see, negative energy is toxic and spreads like a virus; no one is immune from it.

To keep e-mail use in perspective, always remember that *it's not personal—it's business.* Let's start by reviewing some facts about e-mail, some of which may come as a surprise.

E-Mail Facts

Over time, you might feel as if your co-workers have become like family and that you are a permanent part of your organization. That is not the case, so do not let those cozy feelings lead you to letting your guard down, even if you think the director of your agency is your best friend—here is why:

E-mail messages are official documents and
can be used in court cases as evidence.

Always remain aware that your messages can become evidence in legal actions. As a result, your e-mail can also become part of the public domain, as the former employees of Enron discovered. Even casual messages to friends can become evidence in a court case.

Your computer at work is the property of your organization.

Your agency can—and might—monitor your use of e-mail, whether you are aware of it or not. Agencies have the legal right to review any messages that you send or receive. In fact, you have no legal right to privacy for any type of Internet usage while at work, even if you are using a personal e-mail account.

Once you press the send button,
your message is out of your control forever.

Even deleted messages do not go away when they are stored by remote servers. In addition, anyone can forward your message to the director of your agency or a public site: e-mail that you send can go around the world, and you can't stop it. Like any sort of communication, your e-mail message can be twisted and read out of context. And just about anything can go viral in a heartbeat.

Today communication is a global activity, and no one is immune from the entire world's scrutiny. Most people who find themselves immersed in notoriety do not expect it to happen . . . *until after it has happened.* Then life feels unbearably out of control.

By using technology appropriately, you can avoid heartbreaking scenarios. Do not say, post, or do anything that you would not mind having discussed on the national nightly news or a morning talk show, and you will be safe.

E-Mail Guidelines

E-mail does not have rigid rules as compared other types of business correspondence such as letters, memos, reports, and proposals. Though e-mail use continues to evolve, use the following guidelines to keep communications flowing on a professional level:

1. Start your message with a greeting, which creates a personal link between you and your reader, reinforcing the human element of communication.

2. The write the most important information: put purpose up front and clearly state what you need from the reader.

3. Respond to e-mail within one or two days, even if you are simply acknowledging that you are working on the request.

4. Wait about two days after you send a message to follow up on an unmet request or make a phone call.

5. Use an automatic out-of-office response if you will be out of reach for a day or more.

6. Do not copy (Cc) people unless they are in the loop. When people are copied unnecessarily, it wastes their time and can send a negative message that creates an awkward situation.

7. Never use text abbreviations in e-mail: *When in doubt, spell it out.* (When you send a message from a mobile device, make sure a reference such as "Sent from my iPhone" is included so your reader does not expect perfection or even a detailed response.)

8. Press *reply all* only when you are sure that everyone needs to receive your message; when only the sender needs a reply, other recipients become annoyed because it wastes their time.

9. Include a note at the top of a group message that you send stating that only you should receive a reply. Consider developing group lists in which you show the names but not the e-mail addresses of recipients.

10. Forward messages rather than use blind copy (Bcc) when you want to keep people in the loop; this keeps the communication above board.

11. Use standard capitalization: all CAPS (and even bold typeface) can be interpreted as shouting; use all lower case only if you are a techie writing to other techies— otherwise, adapt your writing for your audience.

12. Use an accurate and updated subject line so that your reader can refer to your message and file it easily; include *action needed* in the subject line.

13. Avoid using *read now* and *urgent*; all messages are urgent; demonstrate urgency by using a subject line that includes action needed and a due date.

14. Avoid sending the following types of information via e-mail: confidential, sensitive, or bad news. (Keep in mind that the National Security Agency has been monitoring e-mails.)

15. Encrypt sensitive information such as credit card numbers. (If you do not know how to encrypt information, do a search on "sending sensitive information by e-mail.")

16. Use an *indirect message style* when you must send bad news; however, consider other options before using e-mail.

17. Use visual persuasion so that your reader can pick up key points at a glance; for example, use white space, side headings, bolding, bullet points, and numbering to enhance your message.

18. Number questions and requests so that they stand out.

19. Add a note at the beginning of forwarded messages: explain the action that the reader should take, or let the reader know that the message is only *FYI* (for your information).

20. Leave the history unless you are certain the reader does not need it; deleted history can create frustration and lost time for your reader.

21. Avoid jargon; however, if you use an acronym or initialism, spell it out the first time, putting the abbreviated form in parentheses: "Include your employee identification number (EID)." Or you can use a less traditional approach, flipping the order: "Include your EID (employee identification number)."

22. Avoid slang, and do not use sarcasm; also refrain from sending jokes or being humorous, and use emoticons rarely, if at all. (In a professional message, any kind of slang or sarcasm can cause confusion and miscommunication.)

23. Use e-mail sparingly for personal messages, even if your agency allows it.

24. Avoid sounding suspicious, as in "Delete this message upon reading."

25. Avoid saying, "No, that's not our policy," and instead state what you *can do* for a client.

26. Do not respond to controversial or emotional messages unless you are confident and neutral; better yet, call the person.

27. Do not use "sincerely" as a closing for an e-mail: use "sincerely" exclusively as a closing for formal business letters.

28. Use an informal closing, such as "All the best" or "Best regards."

29. When you use a complete sentence as a closing, end it with a period, not a comma:

  o Take care.

  o Let's talk soon.

  o Thanks for your help.

  o Hope your day goes well.

30. Do not automatically say "thank you" at the end of your message: reserve the use of "thank you" for those times when someone actually helps you with something.

Finally, do not make it a practice to copy people simply to cover yourself as it sends a negative micro-message that contributes to a lack of trust. The e-mail itself is documentation and needs no additional audience.

Social Media

Most social work programs have social media guidelines or policies. Realize that potential employers, field placement sites, and clients may see and read what you post in social media. They can also view your "friends."

Even if you have privacy settings, friends can forward your information to others. Be especially careful about posting pictures of parties and other questionable settings. Use the *National Association of Social Workers Code of Ethics* as a guide.

Your professionalism is always on display. Connecting with clients through social media can create a conflict of interest. Remember what you post reflects on you, the social work program, the agency you may be affiliated with, and the social work profession. *What you post could affect your opportunities and future success.*

E-Time Management

Improving the way that you manage e-mail will save you time and energy. Develop a *system*: a toolbox of decisions that support you in getting your job done. As you review the following, remain open to trying them before you decide they will not work.

1. **Reduce interruptions.** Take back control of your focus and workflow: stop checking your messages *on demand*.

  o Turn off your mail alert indicator.

  o Identify set times to check your messages.

If you need to check messages often, limit yourself to checking once an hour or even once every half hour. When an issue is top priority, the phone is the best solution, regardless of whether you are sending a request of responding to one.

By staying focused on one task, you will achieve more in less time. That is because multi-tasking does not work—your brain can really focus on only one task at a time.

2. **Suggest rather than ask vague or open-ended questions.**

   o If you are scheduling a meeting, offer the reader two or three possible times, adding a comment, "If none of these work for you, let me know a time or two that would."

   o Propose solutions by saying, "I suggest that . . ." or "Would it work for you if the meeting were . . . ?"

3. **Set boundaries.** Identify the issues that drain your energy or time, and be proactive; for example:

   o Do not scan e-mail when you do not have the time to respond.

   o Do not send late-night messages, giving the impression that you have no boundaries and expect others not to have them either.

   o Set a limit for the number of times you exchange messages about a topic before making a phone call—3 or 4 times?

   o When an issue is urgent, make a phone call.

4. **Create folders**. At a minimum, create folders for *action* and *reference*.

   o **Action** messages require a time commitment, which you may need to plan into your day.

   o **Reference** messages add clutter to your Inbox: after you have responded, file them so that you have the history or documentation, as needed.

Here are a few more tips:

- Keep a *to-do list*, using software to keep you organized. Check to see if your e-mail has a calendar and task-list function; you can also do a search for "free software for getting organized."
- Complete challenging tasks at the times when you make your best decisions. For most people, the best time for making decisions is early in the day, before *decision fatigue* sets in.
- Set internal deadlines so that you meet external demands.

Voicemail Messages

When you make a call, you can never be sure that you will reach a person or get voicemail. If you reach voice mail, the last thing you want to do is leave a long, rambling message.

When you leave a message, give your phone number first so it is convenient for your caller to contact you. Here are some guidelines for leaving voice mail messages:

1. Mind map the message before you call.
2. Start your message by stating your name, agency (or connection with the person, such as an academic course or committee you share), and phone number (slowly).
3. Prioritize the information and give the most important details first.
4. Include a time frame: when do you need the information you are requesting?
5. Make sure you include the best times you can be reached.
6. Repeat your phone number *slowly* at the end of the message.

In addition to your phone number, you may also want to provide your e-mail address. By preparing to leave a voice mail *before* you make a call, you will get straight to the point and make it easy for your contact to respond back to you.

Audiovisual Connections

Software such as **Skype** and **Google Hangouts** can connect multiple people who can see each other. **Gotomeetings** also lets you work together on a document, while talking with each other. These tools can help facilitate interactions.

Communication and Relationships

Communication is a human endeavor: at its best, professional communication enhances relationships—don't settle for less. When communication becomes strained, take a step back and reflect on your options *before* you respond.

Do not write it if you would not say it face to face.

When you have done your best and a situation does not seem to be getting better, walk away for a while. Tomorrow is another day, and a good night's sleep refreshes even the worst situation.

When you feel drained of energy and have *decision fatigue*, put off making important decisions or writing sensitive messages. Like everyone else, you do your best work when your mind is clear.

Quick Editing Tips

Though some of the following were covered in previous workshops, you will also find a few more elements of style. This workshop pulls various elements of style together as a quick review. Most of these topics were covered in previous chapters, but some are new.

Control Sentence Structure

The **subject** and **verb** are the core of a sentence. Readers or listeners must hear both the subject and verb of a sentence before they begin to understand its meaning. Putting too many words between the subject and verb complicates the process. Thus, *keeping a subject close to its verb helps the reader understand the message more easily.* In each example below, the subject is underlined once and the verb is underlined twice.

> Jane Addams, a key founder of the social work profession as well as a Nobel Peace Prize winner and advocate for the rights of women and immigrants, co-founded Hull House and the American Civil Liberties Union.

> Jane Addams co-founded Hull House and the American Civil Liberties Union. She was also a key founder of the social work profession, an advocate for the rights of women and immigrants, and a winner of the Nobel Peace Prize.

With the subject and verb closer together, the sentence is easier to read. Breaking the longer sentence into two shorter sentences also makes it more manageable.

Control Sentence Length

Keep sentences between 10 and 25 words in length relates to the amount of information the average reader retains. Beyond 25 words, a reader may find it necessary to reread the beginning of the sentence to understand its meaning. If you find yourself with longer sentences, eliminate words or break up the information into smaller units.

For example:

> Writing experts suggest keeping sentences to fewer than 25 words in length because readers may have difficulty retaining information in longer sentences and may need to read the beginning of a sentence over again if the meaning of the beginning becomes lost by the time the end is reached. (49 words)

Control Sentence Content

Each sentence should have only one controlling idea. When a sentence contains more than one controlling idea, the meaning is not clear.

Weak: The director needs to examine policies about client services, and she is spending her time planning a new fundraiser.

What is this about? Where will it lead? These ideas appear disjointed, but each is given equal weight. You can correct this by showing how the ideas are related.

Revised: Although the director needs to examine policies about client services, she is spending most of her time on the new fundraiser.

Revised: Because the director is spending her time on the new fundraiser, she has not yet examined policies about client services.

Build Old to New Information Flow

Readers can follow your message more easily if familiar ideas lead to unfamiliar ideas. While composing, you may find yourself putting down new ideas (the unfamiliar) and then linking them to your topic (the familiar). When editing, move the familiar idea to the beginning of the sentence and move the unfamiliar idea to the end.

For example, suppose you are sending out a message about an upcoming meeting. As you compose, you may start with the new information.

Weak: The need for new office policies will be the topic of our next meeting.

When you edit, switch the order so the sentence begins with the familiar (meeting):

Revised: At our next meeting, we will discuss the need for new office policies.

By beginning the sentence with the familiar concept (meeting), you ease your readers into the unfamiliar information.

Weak: New procedures will be developed as a result of ongoing problems.

Revised: Because of ongoing problems, we will develop new procedures.

Apply End Stress

The core of a sentence is its subject and verb. After the reader understands the actors and action, information at the end of a sentence stands out. The end becomes the stress point. Thus, emphasize important information by putting it at the end of a sentence.

Weak: At the annual meeting, the <u>award</u> <u>was presented</u> **to George by the director**.

Revised: At the annual meeting, the <u>director</u> <u>presented</u> **the award to George**.

Weak: Our innovative <u>response</u> <u>was appreciated</u> **by their committee**.

Revised: Their <u>committee</u> <u>appreciated</u> **our innovative response**.

When you revise a sentence from passive to active, you may also be moving the new information to the end so that it stands out for the reader.

Use Real Subjects and Strong Verbs

Real subjects and strong verbs create a clear meaning. Here is how to keep your subjects real and verbs strong:

- Use the active voice
- Avoid starting sentences with expletive forms such as "it is" or "there are."
- Use action verbs rather than "state of being" verbs (is, are, seem) and weak verbs (such as make, give, take).
- Eliminate nominals when possible.

<u>There</u> <u>are</u> many clients waiting in the lobby.	Many <u>clients</u> <u>are waiting</u> in the lobby.
<u>It</u> <u>is</u> well <u>known</u> that his preference is golf.	<u>Everyone</u> <u>knows</u> that he prefers golf.
<u>He</u> <u>made</u> everyone aware of the information.	<u>He</u> <u>informed</u> everyone.
<u>We</u> <u>will take</u> that into consideration.	<u>We</u> <u>will consider</u> that.
<u>There</u> <u>are</u> policies that need to be changed.	Some <u>policies</u> <u>need</u> to be changed.
<u>It</u> <u>is</u> her belief that we should present.	<u>She</u> <u>believes</u> that we should present.

Apply Parallel Structure

Parallel structure relates to syntax and clarity. Parallel structure creates balance by presenting related words in the same grammatical form. Make sure that you represent related nouns, verbs, phrases, and clauses in a consistent form. Here are some examples:

Incorrect: The team envisioned a successful future through *strong leadership, making decisions effectively, and new approaches being tried.*

Revised: The team envisioned a successful future through *strong leadership, effective decisions, and new approaches.*

Incorrect: Bob's duties are *surveying* the staff, *prepare* the agendas, and *to chair* the meetings.

Revised: Bob's duties are *surveying* the staff, *preparing* the agenda, *and chairing* the meetings.

Incorrect: The afterschool project grant would have gone smoothly if *reports were prepared on time, we returned their calls,* and *would have included some sort of follow-up.*

Revised: The afterschool project grant would have gone smoothly if *we had prepared reports on time, returned their calls,* and *included some follow-up.*

Parallel structure adds flow through consistency in form. When checking for parallel structure, look for consistent verb tense, word endings, and voice (active or passive).

Avoid Misplaced Modifiers

Modifying words take as their subject the noun closest to them. The writer or speaker always knows the intended meaning, but the reader or listener can be confused, or even amused, by misplaced modifiers. Here are two examples:

Incorrect: Mr. Jones is the person speaking to Susan *with the grey mustache.*

Revised: Mr. Jones is the person *with the grey mustache* speaking to Susan.

Incorrect: Entering the conference room, *John's briefcase* opened and all of his papers fell out.

Revised: As John entered the conference room, his briefcase opened and all of his papers fell out.

EDITING CHECK-LIST

For style, have you incorporated the following principles?

___Control sentence length to 10 to 25 words

___Structure subject and verbs close together

___Control sentence content to one main idea

___ Use the active voice when possible

___ Use the passive voice when appropriate

___ Turn nominals into active verbs

___ Use real subjects and strong verbs

___ Cut empty and redundant words and phases

___ Write in the affirmative

___ Start with old information and lead to new information

___ Use parallel structure

___ Keep modifiers close to the word or words they modify

___ Use conjunctions to show relationships

___ Bridge ideas effectively

Keys to Activities

Workshop 1

Workshop 1 Inventory

The correct answer to all of the questions was 1 (never). If your score was 3 or above, make a special effort to apply process tools as you manage the writing process.

Workshop 2

Workshop 2 Inventory

1. Give substantial background information before stating the purpose. **False**
2. Answering a question starts with understanding the problem. **True**
3. Readers want to know all of the details of *how* you decided on a course of action. **False**
4. Shaping your writing for the audience and its expectations is part of purpose. **True**
5. Three types of information to control are "old," "new," and "empty." **True**
6. A writer's background thinking is considered empty information. **True**
7. Effective paragraphs are coherent, which means that sentences can be about different topics as long as each sentence makes sense. **False**
8. In e-mail messages, your subject line should always reflect your purpose. **True**

Activity 2.1: Analyze the Revision

1. On the revision, "Pam" did not introduce herself by name, which is unnecessary to do in writing. By signing off with your name, you let the reader know who you are.
2. The revised message gets to the point, offering an explanation without giving unnecessary details.
3. The revised message was broken into short paragraphs with white space added.
4. The revised message has an effective closing; reserve the use of "sincerely" for formal letters.

Activity 2.2: Revise for Purpose

The key to this exercise is on page 22.

Activity 2.3: Revise for Cohesion

The *topic sentence* is the first sentence in the paragraph:

By implementing health and safety programs for employees, a corporation can reap multiple rewards. *A comprehensive occupational health program* reduces absenteeism, increases productivity, and improves employee morale. In addition, *a health program* results in substantial savings by reducing insurance claims and premiums.

Remove: Our corporation implemented a health and safety program and had good results. In addition, the families of the employees appreciated the program almost as much as our employees.

Activity 2.4: Revise Information Flow

Our corporation implemented **a health and safety program** and had good results. Our **new program** encouraged employees to take an active role in preventing disease. This **innovative program** provided employees a health center where they could conveniently get daily aerobic exercise and weight training. Another **part of the package** consisted of periodic tests to monitor blood pressure, cholesterol, and triglycerides. Within one year, a significant percentage of employees had reduced risk factors for heart disease.

Remove: Some employees did not set aside time to participate in the program.

Activity 2.5: Summarizing and Paraphrasing

Answers will vary.

Activity 2.6: Revising Sentences

Answers will vary—here are few examples:

1. An incorrect report was accidently sent to you last week by our agency.
    a. Attached is a corrected report; please disregard the previous report as it contained errors, for which we apologize.
    b. The report that you received from us last week was incorrect. Attached is a corrected report. We apologize for any inconvenience this may have caused.
    c. Please accept this correct report to replace the one we previously sent. Thank you for your understanding. Please let me know if you have questions.
2. Your position for a case worker is of interest to me.
    a. Can you tell me more about your position for a case worker?
    b. I am interested in your position for a case worker; attached is my resume.
    c. Would you be available to discuss your position as a case worker? I am interested in the position.

3.   George did not respond to my invitation about joining our committee, so he's probably not interested.

    a.   I'm still waiting to hear from George about whether he is interested in joining our committee.

    b.   I did not hear back from George yet, so I need to follow up with him to see if he's interested in joining our committee.

Application 2.1: Editing E-Mail

Answers will vary.

Application 2.2: Editing Paragraphs

Answers will vary.

Application 2.3: E-Mail Etiquette: Netiquette

Answers will vary.

Workshop 3

Pretest – Workshop 3

1.   If you are unable to attend the meeting, find a replacement immediately.
2.   Should Bob, Jesse, and Marlene discuss these issues with you?
3.   As soon as we receive your application, we will process your account.
4.   Your new checks were shipped last month; therefore, you should have received them by now.
5.   Will you be attending the seminar in Dallas, Texas, on December 15, 2015?
6.   Fortunately, my manager values my efforts and believes in my ability to do quality work.
7.   Mr. Adams, when you have time, please review this contract for me.
8.   We received his portfolio on May 15, and we promptly developed a new strategy.
9.   Carrie brought her report to the meeting; however, it was not complete.
10.   Mr. Jensen sent a letter to my supervisor; the letter was complimentary.
11.   The merger, however, required that each corporation learn to trust the other.
12.   Thank you, Donald, for supporting our quality assurance efforts.
13.   I am not sure about the costs, but I recommend that we consider this proposal.
14.   We received the contract yesterday; however, we have not yet reviewed it.
15.   Mr. Wells will arrive on Wednesday, November 18, as he stated in his letter.

Workshop 3 Inventory

1. Commas are placed in sentences based on pauses. **False**
2. A sentence has a **subject** and a **verb** and expresses a complete thought.
3. A sentence is **b) an independent clause.**
4. Which of the following is a dependent clause:

   b. When your friend arrived.
5. In English, the subject of a sentence generally precedes the verb. **True**
6. Which of the following is not a subordinating conjunction: **d. however**
7. Which of the following is not an adverbial conjunction: **c. if**
8. If a subordinating conjunction such as *if, when,* or *although* is placed at the beginning of an independent clause, the clause will become dependent. **True**
9. Conjunctions signal where to place commas in a sentence. **True**
10. One comma can be correctly placed between the subject and verb of a sentence. **False**
11. The subject and verb are the core of a sentence. **True**
12. Commas are placed based on pauses. ***False!***

Activity 3.1: Comma Practice

1. Before he entered the building, the young man checked the address. INTRO
2. If you would like the agency to process your request, leave your number and a time you can be reached. INTRO
3. George, can I count on your assistance? DA
4. Mr. Jones, the building manager, keeps all of the leases. AP

   Or: Mr. Jones, the building manager keeps all of the leases. DA
5. So that you are able to focus on your meeting, we will hold all calls . . . INTRO
6. After the chairperson made the announcement, the group was in chaos. INTRO
7. In general, we do not include that information on our Web site. INTRO
8. Ms. Whitehead, please e-mail me the information if that is convenient. DA
9. Even though you do not like the referral, it is our only option. INTRO
10. Cathy, when will you inform your task group? DA
11. Please speak to Louise, our assistant, if I am not in the office. AP
12. Although it is important to be on time, it is also important to be prepared. INTRO
13. Until the director arrives, we cannot begin the meeting. INTRO
14. She went to visit her sister in Detroit, Michigan, last year sometime. DA
15. He lists his start date as Friday, September 19, 2007. AD

Activity 3.2: Commas and Semicolons

1. George wanted to go to the conference, but he had a previous commitment. CONJ
2. He had told her about the meeting; she refused to go. NC
3. We, therefore, are sending the material by Federal Express. PAR
4. Mr. Adams gave the statistics, but there were many people who did not believe him. CONJ
   Revise: To improve the sentence, get rid of "there were":
   Mr. Adams gave the statistics, but many people did not believe him. CONJ
5. The issue was resolved once we understood the problem; this was a great relief. NC
   Or: *The issue was resolved; once we understood the problem, this was a great relief.* BC
6. Alexander to went school; Martin preferred to skip school. NC
7. They told us the information too late, so we were not able to attend. CONJ
8. The new printer does not work as effectively as the old one, but it is ours . . .CONJ
9. Mary wants to go to the seminar; however, her supervisor will . . . TRANS
10. Susan did well on the proposal; unfortunately, she was not in the meeting . . . TRANS
11. Mr. Jones never arrives on time; for example, he arrived ten minutes late . . . TRANS
12. The contract states, however, that extended family members can attend . . . PAR
13. Please send the information to George Schmidt; he expected it earlier this week. NC
14. We, therefore, look forward to seeing you on Friday; please call if . . . PAR and NC
15. Bill is a good candidate for that job; he received a recommendation from . . . NC
16. The storm knocked out the power; consequently, the family could not contact us. TRANS

Posttest – Workshop 3

1. We received his letter on May 15, 2014, explaining his concerns. AD
2. Mr. Harris will be here on Tuesday, September 18, as stated in the memo. AD
3. When you have finished, Mr. Harkness, please review this contract for me. DA
4. We received your application yesterday; however, we have not yet had . . . TRANS
5. Unfortunately, my manager does not value my work as much as she should. INTRO
6. I am not sure about the benefits, but I wonder if this approach would be . . . CONJ
7. Will you be attending the conference in Springfield, Illinois, on November 10, 2015? AD and AD
8. Thank you, Ms. Vandergelt, for supporting our efforts. DA
9. Your report was sent on Tuesday; therefore, you should have received it . . . TRANS
10. The proposal, however, required that each agency learn to trust the other. PAR
11. As soon as we receive these documents, we will send you the verification. INTRO
12. Ms. Smith sent a letter to my supervisor; the letter was very complimentary. NC

13. Would you like for Mark, Jodie, and Arlene to bring up these issues with you? SER
14. Della brought her calendar to the meeting, but I forgot mine. CONJ
15. If you are unable to attend the conference, inform your supervisor immediately. INTRO

Workshop 4
Pretest – Workshop 4

1. After Bob had quietly *spoken* his answer, everyone agreed.
2. A social worker said that you *were* unhappy about our service.
3. The pamphlet *included* the information you are looking for.
4. If I *were* you, I would support Tim in his decision.
5. Our acquisition budget is *frozen* until the fourth quarter.
6. Margarite *commended* Albert for the job he does every day.
7. I would've *gone to* the meeting opening if I had been invited.
8. Austin had *given* the report to the committee.
9. You should *have spoken* to their family while the incident was still fresh.
10. Every member of the committee *attended* the conference last June.

Workshop 4 Inventory

1. The subject and verb together form the core of a sentence.   **True**
2. All verbs have both a past tense form and a past participle form.   **True**
3. A helper verb (such as *is, has,* or *do*) must be used with a past participle form.   **True**
4. The verb in a sentence determines its grammatical subject.   **True**
5. For irregular verbs, add *ed* to form both the past tense and past participle.   **False**
6. The base form of a verb is called an infinitive.   **True**
7. All third person singular verbs in English end in *s.*   **True**
8. In the active voice, the *subject, verb,* and *object* perform their prescribed . . . .   **True**
9. A *nominalization* is a noun that originated as a verb.   **True**
10. The subjunctive mood expresses possibility, not fact.   **True**

Activity 4.1: Tense, Agreement, Consistency, and Mood

1. We had finally (did, **done**) our part of the work.

2. He should not have (went, **gone**) to the office on Friday.

3. She (don't, **doesn't**) give that information to ~~no one~~ anyone.

4. She had (spoke, **spoken**) (eloquent, **eloquently**) at the conference.

5. He (loaned, **lent**) me the material for the meeting.

6. You should have (wrote, **written**, writen) to the office first.

7. The phone must have (rang, **rung**) 20 times before they answered.

8. I should (of, **have**) (brang, brung, **brought**) another copy.

9. Who has (**drunk**, drank) the last glass of juice?

10. We were (near, **nearly**) (froze, **frozen**) when they arrived.

11. She should have easily (saw, **seen**) the error in the report.

12. We ate (quick, **quickly**) because we (are, **were**) going to the meeting.

13. They were (took, **taken**) by surprise.

14. She (**has**, have) (chose, **chosen**) the most beautiful graphic.

15. (**May**, Can) I assist you with the project? (Use "may" when you are asking permission; use "can" when you are referring to "ability")

16. They would have (swam, **swum**) if they had more time.

17. My heart (sunk, **sank**) when she gave the news.

18. The budget is (froze, **frozen**) until next quarter.

19. Try (and, **to**) drive more careful.

20. Ever since I (**got**, have) a new manager, I always (got, **have**) too much work.

21. She felt bad because he (is, **was**) not available to assist us.

    Or: She feels bad . . . he was not: *stay in the same tense*

22. That was the most (silliest, **silly**) decision he ever made . . . or, the **silliest**

23. Bob's supervisor was concerned that he (is, **was**) not able to complete the project.

24. He felt (**bad**, badly) about the situation and (wants, **wanted**) to help.

25. She advised him to drive (safe, **safely**) because his new car (runs, **ran**) (bad, **badly**).

26. If I (was, **were**) you, I would (of, **have**) gone to the meeting.

27. I wish she (was, **were**) my client.

28. If Tom (was, **were**) your manager, (will, **would**) you go to the conference?

Activity 4.2: Subjunctive Mood

1. The supervisor requested that Mike (**invite**, *invites*) the new manager to the meeting.
2. John wishes he (*was*, **were**) in charge of the new agency.
3. If Lester (*was*, **were**) on your team, would you support him?
4. It is imperative that she (**complete**, *completes*) the proposal.
5. If Tiffany (*was*, **were**) your manager, (**would**, *will*) you attend the conference?

Activity 4.3: Consistent Tense

1. My manager ~~says~~ *said* we should have gotten the report finished sooner.
2. John gave me the report today because he ~~wants~~ *wanted* to take Friday as a vacation day.
3. Five computer terminals were broken, so the manager ~~is~~ *was* requesting all new ones.
4. My advisor ~~informs~~ *informed* me of class openings, but I signed up for the wrong ones.
5. The program analysis was difficult, and our team ~~requires~~ *required* more time.
6. The inscription on the plaque was blurry and ~~needs~~ *needed* to be corrected.

Activity 4.4: Past Tense

1. Bob finally *indicated* that the information was wrong.
2. The dean *encouraged* me to apply for graduate school.
3. My interview *resulted* in a job offer at another company.
4. Ms. Fielding told me that their agency *merged* with a larger one last year.
5. Have you *planned* for the interview?

Activity 4.5: Active Voice

1. The appointment must have been canceled by one of the clients.

   One of the clients must have canceled the appointment.

2. The check should have been deposited yesterday to avoid an overdraft.

   You should have deposited the check yesterday to avoid an overdraft. (This sentence that would be more effective in the passive voice, the tactful voice.)

3. Your papers should have been sent last week.

   You should have sent your papers last week . . . once again, passive is more tactful.

4. These papers should be filled out and returned by July 15.

   Please fill out and return these papers by July 15.

5. Your request may be approved by the supervisor this week.

   The supervisor may approve your request this week.

6. A copy of the report will be sent to you tomorrow.

   I will send you a copy of the report next week . . . "anyone" can be the subject, but the sentence needs a real subject to perform the action.

7. The check was endorsed by Juan.

   Juan endorsed the check.

8. You and your staff were being praised by everyone for such a great job.

   Everyone praised you and your staff for a great job.

9. Your home telephone number was given to me by your secretary.

   Your secretary gave me your home phone number.

10. You have been given an incomplete report by the human services department.

    The human resources department gave you an incomplete report.

11. There have been many complaints by service recipients about that policy.

    Many service recipients complain about that policy.

12. A new policy for travel reimbursement was implemented by our director.

    Our director implemented a new policy for travel reimbursement.

13. Your assistance will be appreciated by our entire task group.

    Our entire task group will appreciate (or: appreciates) your assistance.

14. The program was cancelled due to lack of interest.

    We cancelled the program due to lack of interest.

    Note: "Someone" must perform the action.

Activity 4.6:Nominalization

1. The director completed the implementation of the dress policy last August.

   The director implemented the dress policy last August.

2. A suggestion was made by our human resource department that meetings be rescheduled.

   The human resource department suggested that meetings be rescheduled.

3. Their broker gave us information about our new insurance policy.

   Their broker informed us about our new insurance policy.

4. Will there be a discussion of the new resource at our next task group meeting?

   Will we discuss the new resource at our next task group meeting?

5. Our director made an announcement about the grant being funded in the October meeting.

   Our director announced that the grant was being funded in the October meeting.

6. The invitation to the conference was given to our department by Alyssa.

   Alyssa invited our department to the conference.

7. Martha's decision about the new computers will be made by Friday.

   Martha will decide about the new computers by Friday.

8. The investigation of the missing computers is being done by Michael.

   Michael is investigating the missing computers.

9. If the assistant would make an adjustment in the schedule, we would have better hours.

   If the assistant would adjust the schedule, we would have better work hours.

10. My supervisor gave a recommendation that I arrive to work on time.

    My supervisor recommended that I arrive to work on time.

Posttest – Workshop 4

1. My supervisor had *spoken* about this policy in a previous meeting.

2. Jessica *said* that you were unable to assist us with this project.

3. The report *includes (or included)* a discussion of our current projects.

4. I would accept the position if I *were* you.

5. We cannot make additional purchases because our budget is *frozen* until next year.

6. Len *addressed* the problem last month.

7. If Margo *would have gone* to the conference, she would have the update.

8. Austin *had given* the report to the committee.

9. You *should've written* about the incident shortly after it happened.

10. Each member of the committee *attends (or attended)* all meetings.

Workshop 5

Pretest – Workshop 5

1. The social worker said that I could contact Bob or ~~yourself~~ *you* for the information.
2. Louise and ~~him~~ *he* selected the location for the meeting.
3. You should let the issue remain between ~~he~~ *him* and your manager.
4. Send the report to Sylvio and ~~I~~ *me* before you send it to the court.
5. A *managers* must inform their employees of benefit changes.
   Or: A *manager* must inform *his or her* employees of benefit changes.
6. If ~~her~~ *she* and her supervisor agree, let's go along with the plan.
7. The counselor sent the report to Bob and ~~I~~ *me*, even though we didn't request it.
8. I like taking classes because it improves ~~your~~ *my* skills.
9. If you have more time than ~~me~~ *I* (do), you should attend the seminar.
10. A project manager should inform others in ~~their~~ *his or her* group about changes.

Workshop 5 Inventory

1. The pronoun *I* can be used as an object at the end of a sentence. **False**
2. Pronouns are categorized by cases, not tenses. **True**
3. For a pair (such as "Bob and I"), to check if using *I* is correct, substitute *we*. **True**
4. Reflexive pronouns can be used as objects or subjects. **False**
5. Pronouns sometimes need to agree with their antecedents. **False**
6. After the conjunction *than,* use a subjective pronoun when the verb is implied. **True**
7. The possessive pronoun *mine* is never made plural by adding an *s*. **True**
8. The pronoun *her's* shows possession. **False**
9. Only use the reflexive pronoun *myself* if it refers back to *I*. **True**
10. A common mistake with pronouns is using *I* when *me* is correct. **True**

Activity 5.1: Pronoun Case

1. John and (**I**, ~~me~~) completed the project yesterday.
2. Barbara was more competent than (**he**, ~~him~~). *Implied verb: "than he was"*
3. Why were the materials delivered to (~~she~~, **her**) and Bob?
4. Dr. Jones said that (~~us~~, **we**) managers should do the work.
5. Between you and (~~I~~, **me**), we have enough expertise. *Follow a preposition with an object; also, substitute the objective case "us" to confirm that "me" is correct*
6. The supervisor required Bob and (I, **me**, myself) to attend the seminar.
7. You can ask George or (I, myself, **me**) for the updated report.
8. They are more competent to do the job than (**we**, us). *Implied verb: "than we are"*
9. The attorney asked that the case be divided among you, Alice, and (myself, **me**).
10. She asked who would do the report, my secretary or (me, myself, **I**). *Or: me*
11. Margaret is busier than (**I**, ~~me~~). *Implied verb: "busier than I am"*
12. Bill likes Sue better than (I, me). See below:

    Either "I" or "me" would work, depending on where the implied verb belongs:

    Bill likes Sue better than I (like Sue).

    Bill likes Sue better than (he likes) me.

13. The professor told my associate and (~~I~~, **me**, ~~myself~~) to complete our report.
14. The information was sent to (~~she and I~~, **her and me**, ~~her and I~~).
15. George and (~~me~~, **I**) watched the podcast before (**he**, ~~him~~) and (**I**, ~~me~~) left.
16. Upon recommendation, he gave the project to Jim and (~~I~~, **me**, ~~myself~~).
17. Bob has more time than (~~me~~, **I**). *Implied verb: "than I have"*
18. The project will be split between John and (~~I~~, **me**, ~~myself~~).
19. She asked Phyllis and (**me**, ~~myself~~) to attend the board meeting.
20. The problem should remain between Bob and (**you**, ~~yourself~~).
21. Did Allison and (**I**, ~~me~~) cause you a problem?
22. I am going to make (~~me~~, **myself**) an excellent dinner.
23. When he asked, I responded, "It is (I, me)." *For formal occasions, use the subjective case after the linking verb "is": "It is I." Otherwise, "It is me" is now considered acceptable.*

Activity 5.2: Pronoun and Antecedent Agreement

1. When an employee calls in sick, they should give a reason.

   An employee . . . he or she; employees . . . they

2. When a social worker does not relate well to their clients, they need more training.

   Social workers . . . their clients . . . they need

3. A social worker is going beyond their job description when they assist a client's guests.

   Social workers are going beyond their job description when they assist their clients' guests.

4. A case manager's job is challenging because they work long hours under difficult conditions.

   Case managers' jobs are challenging because they . . .

5. When a customer does not have a receipt, they may not be able to return an item.

   When customers do not have receipts, they may not be able to return items.

6. Charley said that John should be on his team because he would be available during his training.

   Charley said that John should on his team because Charley would be available during John's training.

7. When a person writes reports, they need to stay focused.

   When people write reports, they need to stay focused.

8. A case manager needs to stay in touch with their clients.

   Case managers need to stay in touch with their clients.

9. When you ask someone for assistance, they should help or let you know they cannot.

   When you ask people for assistance, they should help or let you know they cannot.

10. A person must do their best when the situation calls for it.

    People must do their best then the situation calls for it.

Activity 5.3: Consistent Point of View

1. A supervisor should consider various ways they will deal with personnel problems.

   Supervisors should consider various ways they will deal with personnel problems.

2. One sometimes thinks another situation is better until you experience it.

   You sometimes think another situation is better until you experience it.

3. We generally follow the rules unless you are told otherwise.

   We generally follow the rules unless we are told otherwise.

4. If a person is conscientious, they will do well in their jobs.

   If people are conscientious, they will do well in their jobs.

5. One does not always follow instructions, but we should.

   We do not always follow instructions, but we should.

6. A person should strive to get a great education so you can have a satisfying career.

   People should strive to get a great education so they can have satisfying careers.

7. Trying one's hardest to get in good shape can ruin your health if you're not careful.

   Trying your hardest to get in good shape can ruin your health if you're not careful.

8. Everyone must make their own reservations.

   All attendees must make their own reservations or Make your own reservations.

9. Sue went to the meeting with Mary to ensure that she gave a complete report.

   Sue went to the meeting with Mary to ensure that Mary gave a complete report.

10. Neither of the managers gave their department the memo.

    Neither of the managers gave his (or her) department the memo.

Activity 5.4: Pronoun Consistency

I enjoy working on team projects because **I** learn so much from **my** teammates. **Team members need** to be helpful because they never know when they will need assistance from **their** colleagues. ~~When you are on a team, every~~ All members need to carry their weight. That is, teammates who do not do **their** share of the work can be a burden to the entire team and jeopardize their project.

Team members who stay motivated are more valuable to the team. I always strive to do my best because **I** never know when **I** will need to count on **my** team members.

Note: Answers may vary.

Activity 5.5: Pronoun and Antecedent Agreement

~~A new applicant~~ *New applicants* must understand that ~~you~~ *they* will experience a period of adjustment at their new program. Unfortunately, many new participants think that ~~one's~~ *their* fellow participants should adjust to ~~you~~ *them* instead of the other way around. When ~~you~~ *new participants* begin a new program, ~~one~~ *they* should "lay low" for the first few months to learn the way the work environment functions. After ~~one has~~ *they have* held a position for three or four months, ~~you~~ *they* can begin making appropriate suggestions and changes.

Posttest – Workshop 5

1. You can contact Bob or ~~myself~~ *me* for assistance with the project.
2. ~~Him~~ *He* and his supervisor selected the topic for the conference.
3. Yours are on the table; ~~her's~~ *hers* are in the conference room.
4. You should let the issue remain between ~~he~~ *him* and your co-worker.
5. Send the report to Jeff and ~~I~~ *me* before you pass it on to anyone else.
6. ~~A social worker~~ *Social workers* must inform their clients of the limits to confidentiality.
7. If ~~her~~ *she* and her partner agree, let's go along with the plan.
8. The agency sent the report to Bob and ~~I~~ *me*, even though we didn't request it.
9. You can rely on ~~there~~ *their* instructions in getting the job done effectively.
10. If you have more time than ~~me~~ *I do*, you should attend the seminar.

Workshop 6

Workshop 6 Inventory

1. Complicated, four-syllable words make a writer sound smart. **False**
2. When you request a favor, use the phrase "thank you in advance." **False**
3. To refer to a previous conversation, use the phrase, "per our conversation." **False**
4. Even lawyers should avoid legalese. **True**
5. Certain redundant phrases have been in use for centuries. **True**
6. When attaching a document, use the phrase "attached please find." **False**
7. Background thinking helps readers understand the intent of your message. **False**
8. "Subsequent to" sounds more sophisticated than "after." **False**
9. Simple language is more effective than complicated language. **True**
10. When you use complicated language, it makes you sound smart. **False**

Activity 6.2: Replace Wordy and Outdated Language

1. J -- because
2. C – if
3. E -- about
4. A -- possible
5. F -- while
6. B -- helped
7. L -- believes
8. I – noon or 12 p.m.
9. H -- now
10. G -- always
11. D -- before
12. K – soon

Activity 6.3: Remove Redundancy from Paired Expressions and Modifiers
Answers may vary.

Paired Expressions

~~full and~~ complete

Needless Modifiers

~~free~~ gift

Paired Expressions

true *or* accurate
each *or* every
hope *or* trust
first ~~and foremost~~
various ~~and sundry~~
any *or* all
questions ~~and problems~~
over ~~and done with~~
confusing *or* unclear
forever ~~and ever~~
and so on ~~and so forth~~

Modifiers

~~false~~ pretense
~~true~~ facts
~~future~~ plans
~~personal~~ beliefs
consensus ~~of opinion~~
~~sudden~~ crisis
~~completely~~ finish
~~direct~~ confrontation
~~end~~ result
~~final~~ outcome
~~initial~~ preparation
tuna ~~fish~~

Activity 6.4: Get Rid of Empty, Redundant, and Outdated Language

1. Enclosed please find the papers that were requested by you.

   Enclosed are the papers that you requested.

2. Your complete and absolute confidence in our approach is appreciated.

   We appreciate your confidence in our approach.

3. As per our discussion, the new policy should be received by you this week.

   As we discussed, you should receive the new policy this week.

4. You can completely eliminate one step in the process by using a cover that is green in color.

   You can eliminate one step in the process by using a green cover.

5. I would like to thank you in advance for your consideration of my application.

   Thank you for considering my application.

6. Per your request, the application for admission to our program has been enclosed.

   As you requested, enclosed is the application for admission to our program.

7. The decision for the utilization of that approach with the children was made by your wife.

   Your wife decided to use that approach with the children.

8. Subsequent to their involvement, we made little progress.

   After their involvement, we made little progress. (Or: After they became involved, . . .)

9. Always endeavor to do your best, especially when you are cognizant of the challenges.

   Do your best, especially when you know the challenges. (Or: "are aware of")

10. A free gift has been sent out to you because of your fast and prompt response to our survey.

    We sent you a gift because of your prompt response to our survey. OR: You will receive a gift . . .

11. Per our conversation, we will completely finish the preparations for the June conference by the deadline.

    As discussed, we will finish the preparations for the June conference by the deadline.

12. Attached please find the report, which I am sending per your request.

    Attached is the report that you requested.

Activity 6.5: Editing for Background Thinking

SUGGESTED KEY: *After we spoke, I checked with the supervisor and found out that she has used a similar type of approach with several families.*

Activity 6.6: Editing to Get to the Point

SUGGESTED KEY: *Because of the poor economy, many of our clients will need to reduce their spending. Rather than raising our fees, we should consult with other agencies. What do you think?*

Activity 6.7: Editing to Stay on Point

SUGGESTED KEY: *In reference to your current project, if you are interested in speaking with someone who has encountered similar situations, feel free to contact Cynthia Baker; her number is (123) 555-1234.*

Workshop 7

Workshop 7 Inventory

1. The *you* viewpoint helps you connect more effectively with a client. . . . **True**
2. When you are having a difficult conversation, focus on using the *I* viewpoint. **True**
3. Most negative statements can be made in the affirmative. **True**
4. People respond more positively to statements made in the affirmative . . . **True**
5. The best time to shift to the *you* viewpoint is when you edit. **True**
6. Negative comments are likely to be met with more resistance . . . **True**
7. The *you* viewpoint and affirmative writing have a strong impact on tone. **True**
8. At times, the *I* viewpoint is necessary. **True**

Activity 7.1: The *You* Viewpoint

Answers may vary.

1. I would like to inform you that your input made a difference in our decision.

    Your input made a difference in our decision.

2. We are asking that the completed application be returned within five days.

    Please complete and return the application within five days.

3. I have received your proposal within the deadline.

    Thank you for sending your proposal within the deadline.

4. I would like to invite you to our next team meeting.

    Would you be interested in coming to our next team meeting?

5. I am interested in learning more about your new project.

    Would you tell me more about your project?

6. It seems to me that you are well qualified for the new position.

    You are well qualified for the new position.

7. I respect your opinions and hope to continue to receive them.

    Your opinions are helpful—please continue to offer them.

8. I am hoping to include you on the list of advisors.

    Would you be willing to be an advisor for the new project?

9. I would appreciate if you would do me a favor.

    Would you be willing to do me a favor?

10. I wanted to tell you that I am happy with your new report.

    Your new report is great (excellent, outstanding, and so on).

    Or: You did a great job on your new report.

Activity 7.2: The *You* Viewpoint

Answers may vary.

1. If you wanted your paper to be considered, you should have sent it by the deadline.

    To be considered, your paper should have been sent by the deadline.

2. To avoid an overdraft, you should have deposited funds to your account yesterday.

    Your check should have been deposited yesterday to avoid an overdraft.

3. When you made that remark, you were offensive.

    I felt that the remark was offensive.

Activity 7.3: A Positive Focus

Answers may vary.

1. Do not arrive before noon.

    Please arrive after noon.

2. I don't have time right now.

    If you wish, I could help you with this later today.

3. Here's what happened—J. R. called in sick, and I was shorthanded with lots of other priorities.

    Thank you for your patience; I will be able to complete your project later today.

4. Your credentials do not meet our requirements for the position funded by the grant proposal.

    You have excellent credentials; however, we need someone with more experience for the position.

5. We are behind schedule, and we cannot complete your project by the requested date, July 15.

    We apologize for the delay . . . your project will be completed by July 20. Thank you for your patience.

6. I have not received a response from you for two days, and I need the information now! I know that you carry around an iPhone—why haven't you answered me???

    This is a follow-up to a message I sent the other day. Could you help me by sending the information?

7. When you are late, the meetings don't run smoothly.

    When everyone is on time, the meetings run smoothly.

8. That's not my job—you'll have to speak to someone else.

    I believe that "Katrina" could help you with that. Let me call here . . .

9. No, I can't help you with this—it's our policy that we cannot divulge that type of information over the phone.

    Before that information can be given, we need signed authorization papers.

10. Do not write in the negative.

    Write in the positive (or the affirmative).

Workshop 8

Pretest: Similar Words

1. Will that decision ~~effect~~ you in a positive way? *affect*
2. The ~~principle~~ on my loan is due on the 1st of the month. *principal*
3. My ~~advise~~ is for you to get a job before you buy that new car. *advice*
4. Please ~~ensure~~ my supervisor that I will return in one-half hour. *assure*
5. ~~Its~~ been a challenging day, but things are getting better. *It's*
6. ~~Their~~ are a few issues that we need to discuss. *There*
7. Pat lives ~~further~~ from work than I do. *farther*
8. You can have a meeting ~~everyday~~, if you prefer. *every (single) day*
9. I enjoy working with children more ~~then~~ I enjoy working with teenagers. *than*
10. Megan ~~assured~~ that the project would be successful. *ensured*
11. It's ~~alright~~ for you to contact the social worker directly. *all right*
12. I didn't mean to ~~infer~~ that you were late on purpose. *imply*
13. Try ~~and~~ be on time for the next meeting. *Try to . . .*
14. We wondered ~~weather~~ you ~~where~~ coming. *whether . . . you were*
15. I like your ~~ideal~~ of going to the conference. *idea*

Activity 8.1: Similar Words

1. They have (to, **too**) many new projects and (to, **too**) little time.
2. You will be (appraised, **apprised**) of the situation before noon today.
3. Jackson (**assured**, ensured) me that you got the job.
4. The file documented that she felt (alright, **all right**) about the change.
5. (Your, **you're**) the right person to turn the situation around.
6. (**Among**, Between) the three of us, we have all the resources we need.
7. Try (and, **to**) see Leonard before you leave today.
8. Kevin said that he would (loan, **lend**) me his notes.
9. His remark was a real (complement, **compliment**).
10. The father lives (**farther**, further) from work (**than**, then) the mother does.
11. If you (could of, **could have**) spoken to Della, you'd understand.
12. Vera (past, **passed**) that cold on to her daughters (to, **too**).
13. How will that (**affect**, effect) you?
14. When you know the (affect, **effect**), let me know.
15. Carol (loaned, **lent**) me everything I needed for the meeting.
16. The project lost (**its**, it's) appeal after Mike quit.

17. I (**ensure**, assure) all print materials will be of high quality.

18. After you (ensure, **assure**) me, (**assure**, ensure) the others also.

19. (There, They're, **Their**) boat has left the dock.

20. We are (farther, **further**) along (**than**, then) we realize.

21. Say (its, **it's**) time to go, and we will.

22. If the bank will (loan, **lend**) you enough funds, will you buy the car?

23. My (principle, **principal**) and interest are due on the 1st of the month.

24. That company does all training on (sight, **site**).

25. Did the officer (site, **cite**) you for the violation?

26. When you document your sources, how do you (site, **cite**) a website?

27. We all try to live by our (principals, **principles**).

Activity 8.2: Gender-Neutral and Unbiased Language

Outdated	Revised or Alternative
Policeman	police officer
Waiter/waitress	wait staff or server
Fireman	fire fighter
Stewardess	flight attendant
Mailman	mail carrier
Salesman	sales person
TV anchorman	TV anchor
Mankind	humankind
Chairman	chair person
Housewife	homemaker
Man a project	staff a project

Biased Language	
Schizophrenics	people who have schizophrenia
Challenged	people who have challenges—state the specific challenge
Wheelchair-bound	uses a wheelchair
AIDS victims	people with AIDS
High-risk groups	high-risk behavior
Nonwhite	*state what the population prefers to be called*
Minority	*state what the population prefers to be called*
Blacks	black Americans, African Americans
Senior citizen or oldster	a person who is 65, elderly person

Labels

The elderly or the aged	elderly people
The disabled or the handicapped	people with disabilities
The lower class	people who are poor
The upper class	people with high incomes
The blind	people who are blind
The hearing impaired	people who are hard of hearing or deaf

Hispanic is a term that is sometimes used to represent which specific cultural groups?

Mexican American, Cuban American, Puerto Rican, and sometimes Latino

What other outdated language, biased language, or labels have you encountered? Answers will vary.

Posttest – Chapter 8

1. The ~~affect~~ of their decision is not yet known. *effect*
2. If ~~its alright~~, I'll contact the manager directly. *It's all right*
3. We can meet ~~everyday~~ until we find a solution. *every day*
4. Bob would rather chair a meeting ~~then~~ host a dinner party. *than*
5. When you pay off your ~~principle~~ early, you save on your interest. *principal*
6. My professor gave me good ~~advise~~ about my master's paper. *advice*
7. Take the time to ~~ensure~~ your clients that the change will support them. *assure*
8. ~~Its~~ been a challenging day, but things are getting better. *It's or It has*
9. Giordano's—we are going ~~their~~ for lunch today. *there*
10. On a daily basis, George travels ~~further~~ than I do. *farther*
11. Sam ~~don't~~ know who to trust with this situation. *doesn't*
12. Chuck ~~assured~~ delivery by the due date. *ensured*
13. When you have ~~alot~~ of work, plan your time wisely. *a lot*
14. Starting the meeting late was my ~~ideal~~, not Jan's. *idea*
15. Try ~~and~~ create a positive tone from the beginning of the meeting. *Try to*

Workshop 9

Pretest – Chapter 9

1. Ms. Amanda Wittfield, *director of our company*, will attend the meeting.
2. The *women's* comments were not taken as they were meant.
3. *Paul and Mary's* file was in the wrong cabinet.
4. You can ask Trent Olsen, the new *vice president of marketing*.
5. Our *agency's* mission is to assist young people.
6. Send me a copy of your new book, *Finding a Job in 30 Days*.
7. Her *assistant's* response was that he could not do the work.
8. The *men's and women's* responses were recorded by the assistant.
9. The *speaker's* remark sparked the *audience's* laughter.
10. *It's* all in a *day's* work!

Workshop 9 Inventory

1. Capitalize common nouns that sound proper.   **False**
2. Always capitalize a person's official job title.   **False**
3. When a regular noun is plural and possessive, place the apostrophe after the *s*.   **True**
4. Capitalize business titles only when they immediately precede a name.   **True**
5. Proper nouns are always capitalized, but proper adjectives are not.   **False**
6. For irregular plural possessives, add an apostrophe plus *s*.   **True**
7. To understand capitalization, you must first know the difference between a common noun and a proper noun.   **True**

Activity 9.1: Possession and Word Order

1. the friends of my brother — my brother's friends
2. the cover of the book — the book's cover
3. the end of the day — the day's end
4. the influence of the team leader — the team leader's influence
5. the leaders of our nation — our nation's leaders
6. the advice of my professor — my professor's advice
7. the reports of the agency — the agency's reports
8. the success of our team — our team's success
9. the color of the file — the file's color
10. the work of one day — one day's work

Activity 9.2: Singular and Plural Possessives

1.	supervisor	my supervisor's office	both supervisors' offices
2.	teacher	this teacher's table	these teachers' tables
3.	year	this year's schedule	both years' schedules
4.	assistant	my assistant's laptop	our assistants' laptops
5.	student	the student's speech	two students' speeches
6.	letter	a letter's address	these letters' addresses
7.	client	the client's needs	all client's needs
8.	child	the child's file	both children's files
9.	social worker	a social worker's plan	two social workers' plans
10.	supervisor	a judge's ruling	many judges' rulings
11.	person	a person's integrity	several people's integrity
12.	woman	a woman's idea	many women's ideas

Activity 9.3: Possessives Standing Alone

1. *Ambra and Lucia's* instructor *refuses* to let them work together.
2. Either *Alexi's* report or *Basma's* will persuade the judge.
3. Milton suggested that we go to *Ditka's for* the meeting.
4. My *brother-in-law's* attorneys opened their office last week.
5. *Chandra and her partner's* office *needs* to be remodeled.

Activity 9.4: Possessive Review

1. The report was given at last *week's* meeting.
2. The *department's* duties were *changed* dramatically.
3. When she spoke, everyone was aware it was *Bob's* error.
4. The supervisor wanted to change the *meeting's* location.
5. The *director's* assistant was rude.
6. A *week's* time had *passed* before we noticed the change.
7. The manager spoke highly of both *Jim's* and *Robin's* reports. (*two separate reports*)
8. There *are* few people who know the *report's* real recommendation.
9. *Alice's* remark was very similar to *George's (remark)*.
10. When she *asks too* many *questions,* her *team's* attitude *changes*.
11. The reports *were* in *Mr. Jones'* office.
12. When we arrived, we looked for *Joe and Margie's* report. (*a shared report*)

Activity 9.5: Capitalization Review

1. The director of social services, Phillip James, called the client. (no change)
2. Have you taken enough *English* and math to meet the requirements?
3. The *Federal Government* employs thousands of people.
4. Many federal employees appreciate that benefit. (no change)
5. Will *Professor Davis* hold a *make-up* session?
6. Are you majoring in social work? If so, take *Social Work 421* next semester.
7. Note: *All* proposals are due by the first of the month.
8. You can ask your professor about the project; would that be *Professor* Martinez?
9. The director of our agency said, "*We* are due for important change."
10. Did *Professor* Ford attend the convention?
11. We love to visit *European* cities when we travel.
12. Yesterday the director of social services, Julia McGregor, revealed her plans. (no change)
13. Yesterday *Director of Social Services* Julia McGregor revealed her plans.
14. Yesterday Julia McGregor, director of social services, revealed her plans. (no change)
15. Our social worker, Sylvia Hines, is taking the case. (no change)
16. The counselor asked, "*Would* you like another copy of *NASW's Code of Ethics*?"
17. When you receive your *bachelor's* degree, will it be a *Bachelor of Science in Social Work*?
18. If you can, work on your *master's* degree, get a *Master of Science in Social Work.*

Activity 9.6: Capitalizing Book and Article Titles in APA Style

1. **Book Title:** Research with Human Subjects
   In text: *Research with Human Subjects*
   Reference: *Research with human subjects*

2. **Book title:** Helping Skills for Social Workers
   In text: *Helping Skills for Social Workers*
   Reference: *Helping skills for social workers*

3. **Article title:** The Implementation of the Patient Protection and Affordable Care Act
   In text: The author criticized the article "The Implementation of the Patient Protection and Affordable Care Act,"
   Reference: The implementation of the Patient Protection and Affordable Care Act

4. **Article title:** Projects: A Key to Student Learning

   In text: "Projects: A Key to Student Learning"

   Reference: Projects: A key to student learning

5. **Website title:** Patient Protection and Affordable Care Act

   In text: The HealthCare.gov website "Patient Protection and Affordable Care Act" . . .

   Reference: Patient Protection and Affordable Care Act

6. **Website title:** Strengthening Your Writing Skills: An Essential Task for Social Workers

   In text: One of the most helpful websites was "Strengthening your writing skills: An essential task for social workers."

   Reference: Strengthening your writing skills: An essential task for social workers

Posttest –Chapter 9

1. Amanda will complete her *bachelor's degree in social work* this fall.

   Capitalize the full degree: Bachelor of Science in Social Work

2. The *children's* toys were scattered around the play room.

3. I have taken several classes in social work this year.

   Note: "social work" is not a proper noun.

4. My favorite class was *Writing in the Field, Social Work 270.*

5. The professor of the class is *director of child services.*

6. He recommended reading the book *How to Find a Job in 30 Days.*

7. When you receive your *master's in social work*, you can put MSW after your name.

8. Mary received her *bachelor's degree* last year and is now working on her *master's.*

9. Every time that *I* tried to assist the client, she refused my help.

10. *It's* all in a *day's* work!

Workshop 12

Workshop 12 Inventory

1. A PowerPoint (PP) presentation should tell "the whole story." **False**
2. In general, rich designs are preferred over simple designs for PP slides. **False**
3. Which type of font is recommended for PP slides:

   a. serif   ***b. non-serif***
4. Especially complicated information should be presented on slides. **False**
5. To make slides easier to read, use acronyms and abbreviations. **False**
6. Limit the amount of text to no more than fifteen words per line. **False**
7. Put up to 15 lines as long as you reduce your font size. **False**

E-Mail Inventory

1. To save time, the best way to manage e-mail is to read "on demand." **False**
2. When conveying bad news, it is best to get to the point. **False**
3. Some messages have an emotional overtone and should be responded to in the same kind of tone. **False**
4. In general, give an explanation before stating the main point. **False**
5. For urgent messages, e-mail is the best communication option. **False**
6. Respond to all e-mail messages within a day or two, even when you have doubts about your message. **False**
7. E-mail messages are legal documents. **True**
8. An indirect purpose of professional communication is to:

   a. inform   b. persuade   ***c. build client relationships***
9. When you don't want to speak to someone, e-mail is your best option. **False**
10. Have you ever sent an e-mail message that you wish you hadn't sent? (*Most people have* :)

Notes

Made in the USA
San Bernardino, CA
12 May 2018